"For deacons who want to fulfill their liturgical role with more faith and understanding, for those who wonder what deacons may and may not do, for those curious about the history of the diaconate, for priests who share responsibilities with deacons, for men considering a call to the diaconate, for anyone seeking a better view of what deacons do and who they are, Deacon Frederick Bauerschmidt offers sure-footed information, pastoral guidance, and inspirational confidence."

> —Rev. Paul Turner
> Pastor, St. Anthony Catholic Church, Kansas City, MO
> Author, *Let Us Pray: A Guide to the Rubrics of Sunday Mass*

"Deacon Frederick Bauerschmidt deals in very practical terms with the multifaceted aspects of the deacon's liturgical ministry, but also with the spirituality of his service. There is a superb balance struck between attending to the 'situational awareness' of the liturgy and the deacon's prayerful participation. Quite simply, *The Deacon's Ministry of the Liturgy* is splendid and I cannot recommend it highly enough."

> —Deacon Owen F. Cummings
> Academic Dean and Regents' Professor of Theology
> Mount Angel Seminary

The Deacon's Ministry of the Liturgy

Frederick C. Bauerschmidt

LITURGICAL PRESS
Collegeville, Minnesota

www.litpress.org

1   2   3   4   5   6   7   8   9

Library of Congress Cataloging-in-Publication Data

Names: Bauerschmidt, Frederick Christian, author.
Title: The deacon's ministry of the liturgy / Frederick C. Bauerschmidt.
Description: Collegeville, Minnesota : Liturgical Press, 2016. | Series: The deacon's ministry
Identifiers: LCCN 2015040839| ISBN 9780814648230 | ISBN 9780814648483 (ebook)
Subjects: LCSH: Deacons—Catholic Church. | Catholic Church—Liturgy without a priest.
Classification: LCC BX1912 .B345 2016 | DDC 264/.02—dc23
LC record available at http://lccn.loc.gov/2015040839

For
Deacon Frank Hodges
and
Dr. Cyndi Tifft,
devoted servants of the church's liturgy.

Contents

Chapter 1

The Deacon and the Liturgy in Scripture and Tradition   1
   Liturgy and Deacons in Scripture   1
   Deacons in the Liturgy of the Early Church   4
   Deacons in the Liturgy of the Middle Ages   9
   Deacons in the Liturgy from the Reformation to Vatican II
    and Beyond   13

Chapter 2

Building Blocks of Liturgical Ministry   17
   Ritual and Sign   17
   Serving   19
   Presiding   20
   Moving   22
   Speaking   24
   Singing   26
   Secondary Matters: Positioning, Vesting, Censing   28

Chapter 3

The Eucharist   31
   The Introductory Rites   32
   The Liturgy of the Word   35
   The Liturgy of the Eucharist   40
   The Concluding Rites   48

Chapter 4

Christian Initiation   50
   Christian Initiation of Adults   50
   The Baptism of Children   58

Chapter 5

Making Holy Our Days   69
    The Liturgy of the Hours   69
    Sunday (and Other) Celebrations in the Absence of a Priest   72
    Eucharistic Exposition and Benediction   76

Chapter 6

Making Holy Our Years   79
    Advent-Christmas   80
    Lent-Easter   81
    Saints' Days   90

Chapter 7

Making Holy Our Lives   92
    Weddings   92
    Ordinations   98
    Ministry to the Sick and Dying   99
    Rites for the Dead   101

Chapter 8

Liturgy and the Spiritual Life of the Deacon   107
    The Spirituality of Liturgical Ministry   107
    Praying the Liturgy of the Hours   109
    A Liturgically Shaped Space Within   112

Notes   115

CHAPTER 1

The Deacon and the Liturgy in Scripture and Tradition

For Catholics, our theological reflection ought to be rooted in Scripture as read in light of the tradition with the guidance of the church's teaching office. It is therefore fitting that, as we begin to explore the deacon's ministry of liturgy, we look to Scripture and tradition for insight both into the nature of liturgy and the role of the deacon within it. From this starting point we can begin to understand not simply *what* the deacon does in the liturgy, but *why* he does what he does, for it is only if the deacon is firmly grounded in the history and theology of the liturgy that he will be able to carry out his ministry of liturgy well.

Liturgy and Deacons in Scripture

The most ordinary meaning of the term "liturgy" is the more-or-less set ritual forms of public worship employed by practitioners of the different religions of the world. In the ancient Greek-speaking world, however, *leitourgia* was a public work or act of service to the city or *polis*, typically undertaken by a person of means at his own expense (often as an alternative to paying taxes). This might include providing a chorus for a festival, financing athletic competitions, or providing a military vessel in time of war.[1] Though not excluding religious service, since festivals and plays often had a religious element, the meaning of the term was broad enough to include a number of "public works" projects that we would consider secular.

This term was already taken over by the scholars who translated the Hebrew Scriptures in the third century BC, who used it to refer to the ritual service rendered by the Levites in the temple.[2] It is worth noting that the Levites were not priests, but those who assisted the priests at the sacrifice, and thus were seen in the Christian tradition as precursors of the diaconate. Here, the meaning of *leitourgia* seems to indicate a religious work, but one that is undertaken for the good of the community as a whole. The "public work" of the Levites was their ritual service in the temple.

This religious sense of *leitourgia* is carried over into Luke's gospel, where it is used to refer to Zechariah's ritual priestly service in the temple (Luke 1:23). Other New Testament texts also use the term, or closely related terms, to refer to priestly or other religious service. The letter to the Hebrews says that Christ's *leitourgia* is more excellent than that exercised by the priests in the temple, referring to their role of performing the sacrificial ritual (Heb 8:6). It also speaks of the angels as *leitourgika pneumata*—sometimes translated "ministering spirits"—which refers to the assistance they offer people on earth, but may also be a reference to their role in the heavenly worship of God (Heb 1:14). In the letter to the Romans, Paul says that he has been given grace to be the *leitourgon* to the Gentiles by "ministering-in-a-priestly-way" (*hierourgounta*) to the gospel, though it is not clear that he is referring to any sort of ritual ministry (Rom 15:16). Other uses in Paul seem clearly non-ritual, such as his *leitourgia* of providing a collection for the poor in Jerusalem, though we ought not to forget that this collection might well have been collected as part of the Christians' gathering for worship (2 Cor 9:12). In all of these uses we can hear echoes of the secular Greek sense of "liturgy" as something that one does as a "public work" for the good of one's community.

Apart from explicit uses of the term "liturgy," the Scriptures also presume the ritualized worship of God. The Old Testament bears ample witness of the "liturgical" nature of Israelite worship, both in the meticulous descriptions of what took place in the temple and in the psalms, which give us many of the texts used in Israelite worship. Sometimes people think that the Christian rejection of the Jewish ceremonial law as a vehicle for salvation meant that Christians rejected all sense of ceremony and ritual, but both Jesus and the churches of the New Testament presume much of the liturgical life of Israel as a backdrop. Early Christian worship, while not approaching the temple in splendor, was characterized neither by freewheeling unstructured enthusiasm nor by puritanical sobriety. We can safely presume that at the Last Supper Jesus followed the traditional pattern of Jewish sacred meals and that these ritual meals carried over as the fundamental framework within which the early Christian Eucharist developed. Baptism, associated with dying and rising in the Pauline tradition (Rom 6:3-4; Col 2:12) and with birth in the Johannine tradition (John 3:5), was clearly an action carried out with a sense of ritual awe. Moreover, St. Paul, in writing to the Corinthians, expresses his desire that, when Christians gather for worship, all things "be done properly and in order," meaning that exuberant expressions of the Spirit's presence not overwhelm the set pattern of worship (1 Cor 14:40).

Does Scripture give us any insight into the role of deacons in these early Christian assemblies? The short answer is no, not directly. Some, interpreting the seven chosen in Acts 6 as the first deacons, have wanted to see some sort of liturgical ministry in their being set apart "to serve at table" (Acts 6:2), but this is not clear. It is possible that this "serving" took place at the Christian communal meal, which was not yet clearly distinct from the Eucharist, but the term could also mean simply keeping the community's accounts. One of the seven, Philip, baptizes an Ethiopian eunuch, which could certainly be considered a liturgical action (Acts 8:36-38). But even if we do see the seven as the first deacons, which some scholars dispute, we cannot know whether or not Philip's action tells us something about what was normal for deacons. The First Letter to Timothy tells us something about the qualifications for the office of deacon, but nothing significant about its role, liturgical or otherwise.

We might also look at the word *diakonia* for hints concerning the role of those who took their name from this term. It is usually translated as "service" or "ministry." Modern scholars have tended to treat this as a term that implies a kind of lowliness or humility, but more recently it has been suggested that in secular Greek a *diakonos* was not just any sort of servant, but one who acted on behalf of his or her master—an agent or go-between. John Collins notes that though the various forms of the word *diakonia* found in the New Testament cannot be reduced to a single meaning, wherever it is found it "will always connote a mandate from a commissioning person or institution."[3] Rather than simply being a humble servant, one who engaged in *diakonia* might well have exercised a certain kind of leadership: a leadership carried out on behalf of another, an authority that arises from being authorized. This in itself does not tell us how those called deacons functioned liturgically in the first century, but it might help us understand why deacons functioned the way that they did as the church developed in subsequent centuries.

In short, there is much that we do not know about Christian worship in the first century, and even more of which we are ignorant concerning deacons and their roles. We can presume that Christian gatherings had at least in part a ritual character and that the emerging office of deacon has some role in those assemblies, but the exact nature of that role is, as far as we know, lost to history.

Deacons in the Liturgy of the Early Church

The amount of our information on deacons and the liturgy increases as we move through the first few centuries of the church. One of the earliest Christian documents outside of the New Testament, the *Didache*, which may date from the late first century, gives us a little more information on Christian worship, including instructions on how to baptize and prayers for use at the Eucharist. After instructing Christians to gather on the Lord's Day (i.e., Sunday) "to break bread and to give thanks,"[4] the *Didache* immediately goes on to say, "appoint for yourselves bishops and deacons," but does not specify any particular liturgical duties for them, describing them only as "prophets and teachers."[5] Writing at the first decade of the second century, Ignatius of Antioch (died ca. 110) speaks of deacons as "servants of the mysteries of Jesus Christ," and notes, "they are not servants of food and drink but servants of the Church of God."[6] Perhaps we have here an allusion to the Eucharist and the deacon's role within it, but what that role is we cannot say. Writing in Rome in the middle of the second century, Justin Martyr (100–165) gives us our earliest account of what at least one Christian community did when it assembled on the Lord's Day: reading the Scriptures, listening to preaching, making intercession for the world, taking bread and wine, giving thanks over them, and receiving them as the Body and Blood of Christ. In the course of this description Justin makes explicit mention of the role of the deacon in distributing the Eucharist to the assembly, as well as carrying it to those who are absent.[7]

More evidence accumulates in the third and fourth centuries. In North Africa, Tertullian (ca. 155/160–after 220) mentions that deacons and presbyters can baptize if they have the permission of the bishop.[8] Writing slightly later, Cyprian of Carthage (ca. 200–258) says that presbyters celebrating the Eucharist should do so with the assistance of a deacon[9] and mentions explicitly the deacon's role of administering the cup.[10]

Even more detail can be found in the document that modern scholars have called the *Apostolic Tradition of Hippolytus*, but which recent research indicates may be a composite document dating from a number of different places, including perhaps Rome and Egypt, and times, ranging from the mid-second to the mid-fourth centuries.[11] The text provides a prayer for use at the ordination of deacons that describes them as chosen "to present in your sanctuary the offering of him who was established as your high priest, to the glory of your name."[12] This fits with descriptions elsewhere in the text of deacons presenting the bread and wine to the bishop at the altar prior to the eucharistic prayer.[13] Deacons, along with presbyters, helped in the breaking of the bread for Communion,[14] but, in a practice different from what we saw in Cyprian, only helped distribute Communion by ministering the cup if insufficient presbyters were present.[15] Apart from the Eucharist, deacons also had an assisting role at baptism: they held the oil of exorcism for the pre-baptismal anointing and the chrism (called the oil of thanksgiving) for the post-baptismal anointing; they also went down into the font with the candidate, and may have performed the actual baptismal immersions.[16] In the absence of the bishop, deacons could also preside at the evening agape meal, which involved distributing a blessed cup and blessed bread (in that order) to those who were assembled.[17]

From the Christian East, the third-century Syrian document known as the *Didascalia* fills out some other liturgical roles of deacons. In particular, it points to the role of the deacon in keeping order in the liturgical assembly. One deacon stood at the door as a porter, controlling who came in and making sure that they went to sit in their proper places, which was strictly defined by age and sex. Another stood inside, "next to the gifts for the Eucharist" (presumably the bread and wine that were to be consecrated), and made sure that everyone remained in his or her proper place, admonishing them if they were mislocated. He was to make sure as well "that no one whispers, falls asleep, laughs, or nods."[18] The deacon also had the role of initiating the kiss of peace before the eucharistic prayer by saying in a loud voice, "Does anyone have something against another?"[19] Perhaps he asked this because he was the one who had been scrutinizing everyone during the Liturgy of the Word. This role of the deacon as liturgical "enforcer" is also reflected in a slightly later document originating from Egypt, probably in the fourth century, known as *The Canons of Father Athanasius*, which notes, "if any of the people should talk loudly, the presbyter is to blame the deacons for this since the latter have not trained the people."[20] In this document, deacons were not only charged with restraining an unruly assembly; they also had to restrain themselves: "As to the deacons who strike one another at the altar [. . .], they must stand outside [the church] for a month and fast for a week."[21]

Another document from the East, the fourth-century *Apostolic Constitutions*, shows deacons doing a variety of tasks during the celebration of the Eucharist, many of which are familiar to this day: reading the gospel (a task shared with presbyters);[22] leading the litany of intercession "for the whole Church, for the whole world and for its various parts, for the products of the earth, for priests and rulers, for the bishop, for the sovereign, and for peace everywhere";[23] preparing the offering;[24] ministering the cup at Communion;[25] and dismissing the people.[26] Some duties might seem less familiar, such as expelling penitents[27] or fanning the offerings to keep bugs away.[28] At the same time, certain things are explicitly forbidden to deacons: "The deacon is not allowed to offer sacrifice, to baptize, to give a blessing whether it be small or large."[29]

This concern over clearly distinguishing diaconal roles from presbyteral and episcopal ones and asserting the superiority of presbyters over deacons began to emerge at least as early as the Council of Nicaea (325), which had forbidden deacons from giving Communion to presbyters—"neither the canon nor custom permits Christ's Body to be distributed to those who offer the sacrifice by those who cannot offer it"—and enjoining deacons to "remain within the limits of their functions and remember that they are servants of the bishops and are subordinate to the presbyters."[30] In the East, the so-called *Canons of Hippolytus*, dating from the fourth or fifth century, noted that the deacon should distribute Communion only if the bishop or presbyter explicitly tells him to do so.[31] Even when the deacon brings Communion to a presbyter who is sick, the presbyter is to receive it at his own hands and not from the deacon.[32] In the West, the Second Synod of Arles, held in the second half of the fifth century, forbade deacons from sitting with the priests and from distributing the Eucharist when a priest was present.[33] Pope Gelasius (died 496) warned that "deacons are to observe their proper limits" and that "their service is to include nothing that antiquity has properly assigned to the higher orders."[34]

Some writers attempted to distinguish diaconal and presbyteral roles by presenting them as complementary rather than competitive. An anonymous fifth-century treatise titled *De Septem Ordinibus Ecclesiae* noted:

> The priest is commanded to pray, the deacon to sing psalms. The priest is to sanctify the offerings, the deacon to distribute what has been sanctified. Priests should not presumptuously take the cup from the Lord's table unless it has been handed to them by a deacon. [. . .] Deacons place the offerings on the altar. They arrange the Lord's table. Deacons assist the priest while the sacraments are blessed. Deacons pray before the priest prays. [. . .] The Lord granted us the diaconal order so that all might see that the priest is not the only minister who acts and performs in church. The priest needs the diaconal office just as the deacon needs the priestly office, much the same as there can be no rich person without a poor person, nor someone poor without someone rich. [. . .] The presbyter needs a chair, the deacon an altar, the subdeacon the sacristy, the reader a lectern, the doorkeeper a church, and the grave digger a cemetery. [. . .].[35]

Here the diversity and mutual dependence of liturgical ministers—not simply presbyters and deacons but also subdeacons, lectors, and so forth—served as a reminder of human interdependence more generally. The liturgy, in the coordinated harmony of its ministries, was an image of the coordinated harmony of God's kingdom.

One area where friction over the liturgical role of deacons showed itself most clearly was in baptism. Despite the example of Philip and the Ethiopian eunuch in Acts 6, there was disagreement as to the circumstances under which a deacon could baptize. The *Testamentum Domini*, a church manual written in the fourth or fifth century in what is today Turkey, stated that deacons could only baptize in cases of necessity when a presbyter is not present.[36] An Armenian synod held in 527 likewise restricted deacons from baptizing except in cases of necessity.[37] In the West, Pope Gelasius, in a letter written in the late fifth century, took a position, similar to what we see in the East, that deacons should baptize only in extreme emergencies and "may do what lay Christians commonly do"—that is, administer emergency baptism.[38] Other Western writers, however, saw diaconal administration of baptism as more normal. Writing a century before Gelasius, Jerome (ca. 345–420) seemed not to put any restriction on deacons baptizing.[39] A few decades after Gelasius the Second Synod of Orleans (533) treated baptism as an ordinary part of diaconal ministry, directing that no one be ordained as a priest or deacon who does not know how to baptize.[40] Particularly striking is the strong statement in *De Septem Ordinibus Ecclesiae* that "no one can believe that a person baptized by a bishop is more holy than a person baptized by a deacon."[41] As we move into the Middle Ages, the differences in Eastern and Western approaches solidify, with deacons in the West tending to be seen as ministers of the sacrament of baptism in nonemergency situations and those in the East baptizing only in emergency situations. A similar difference develops with regard to deacons administering Communion, with some of the churches of the East restricting this to bishops and presbyters, which was not the case in the West.[42]

One general development of the patristic period, especially after Emperor Constantine legalized Christianity in AD 312 and began to function as a patron of the church, was the increasing splendor of the setting of the liturgy. Elements of civic ritual were carried over into the liturgy, especially the practice of the bishop being preceded in procession by candles and incense, just as Roman civic officials were. Processions both within and outside churches became very prominent and popular. Music grew more elaborate and deacons were often highly prized for their singing ability, so much so that Pope Gregory the Great in the late sixth century decreed:

> It has long been customary in the Roman church to ordain cantors as deacons, and, furthermore, to use them for singing rather than for preaching and caring for the poor. As a result at divine services a good voice is more appreciated than a good life. Consequently no deacon may henceforth sing in the church except for the gospel at Mass. The remaining lessons and psalms shall be sung by subdeacons or, if necessary, by those in minor orders.[43]

Clergy also adopted formal attire for the liturgy that was originally the same as secular formalwear but, as fashions changed, came to be seen as distinctively sacred garments, reserved for liturgical purposes and bearing symbolic value.[44] Writing in the fifth century, Theodore of Mopsuestia remarked on the deacon's vestments, which "make them seem more impressive than they are." At the same time he noted that the deacon's way of wearing the stole—on the left shoulder and hanging down in front and back—was both a sign of service and "the sign of the freedom to which all of us believers in Christ have been called."[45]

By the end of the sixth century, the liturgy had taken a form that in many ways would be recognizable to us today. Similarly, the ministry of the deacon within the liturgy was fairly well defined, including his role as reader of the gospel, leader of the intercessions, and exhorter of the assembly—all roles that still today form part of the liturgical ministry of deacons.

Deacons in the Liturgy of the Middle Ages

The line between late antiquity and the early Middle Ages is a fuzzy one. Indeed, it is a division that was only drawn in retrospect, by later historians, and many elements from the first centuries of Christianity carried over into the period that followed the demise of the Roman Empire. Yet often historians of the liturgy see this thousand-year period as an undifferentiated era of decline, in which the liturgy came to be seen less as something in which all of the faithful played a part and more as a sacred drama staged by the clergy for the benefit of an essentially passive assembly.[46] While there is an element of truth in this picture, the reality is, as is so often the case, more complicated. In this section, I will look first at some broad trends in the liturgical developments of this period and then look specifically at what happened to the liturgical role of the deacon.

Perhaps the most significant changes in how Christians experienced the liturgy during the Middle Ages is related to language. In the West, Latin was the language of literacy, and so the liturgy, because it was increasingly fixed in texts, remained in Latin. The people of northern Europe, however, spoke a variety of Germanic languages, and in southern Europe spoken Latin was rapidly evolving into early versions of the Romance languages we know today. In some sense, then, the language of the liturgy became a barrier to the participation of many of the faithful. But the issue is more complex than it might first appear. Particularly in southern Europe, where people spoke vernaculars derived from Latin, many of the laity apparently had some *passive* ability to understand Latin; where their difficulty arose was in their *active* ability to speak Latin (not unlike how an English-speaker today might be able to understand Shakespeare but would be hard put to write grammatically correct sixteenth-century prose). In terms of participation in the liturgy, this meant that the faithful might be able to identify what the gospel reading was or to make some of the shorter, fixed responses (e.g., *Et cum spiritu tuo*), but were not capable in joining in longer hymns or prayers of the liturgy, which were increasingly taken over by clerical choirs.[47] In the late thirteenth century, a local church council in Italy decreed that deacons should not use overly elaborate chants for the gospel since this would impede the people's understanding of what was being sung, which indicates that even at this late date there was some expectation, at least in Italy, that the laity could understand at least some of the words of the liturgy.[48] So while the level of vocal participation by the laity undoubtedly decreased over the course of the Middle Ages, this should not be taken to mean that they suffered a total alienation from the action of the liturgy.

To the degree that the spoken language of the liturgy formed a barrier to lay participation, this was partially overcome by the rich ceremony of the liturgy itself, which engaged the senses and the imagination. We should not underestimate the sheer sensual appeal of the liturgy—with its brilliantly colored vestments and windows and statuary, its fragrant incense, its sonorous chanting—particularly in a world that was not saturated with bright imagery and recorded music in the way that ours is. In addition, allegorical interpretations of the various rites, such as those offered by Amalar of Metz in the mid-ninth century, correlated the action of the liturgy to events in the life of Jesus, serving both the didactic purpose of teaching the life of Christ through the liturgy and the spiritual purpose of helping worshipers affectively engage the liturgical action.

Some have noted that even if people were engaged, it was primarily as individuals: robbed of their common voice in the liturgy, the assembly disintegrated into a mere collection of people using the liturgy as a backdrop for their private devotions. Most significantly, beginning already in the fourth century in the East and spreading to the West in the early Middle Ages, the frequency with which laypeople received Communion at Mass declined drastically, until the Fourth Lateran Council (1215) had to mandate that the laity receive Communion once a year at Eastertime in order to retain their good standing in the church. Not only the vocal participation of the laity, but also the ultimate sign of the collective unity of the church, the assembly's communion, largely disappeared from the liturgy.

Yet more recent scholarship has pointed out the ways in which the liturgy was understood in profoundly communal terms in the Middle Ages; rather than being a pageant enacted by the clergy for a passive lay audience, it was a sacred drama in which all were involved and that enacted what the historian John Bossy calls "the social miracle" that created a space of "public holiness where the parish could assemble together to combine sociability with the worship of God."[49] Above all, the celebration of the Mass, even with the infrequent communion of the laity, was a powerful experience of being bound together through the blood of Christ shed on the cross. Controversy over the teachings of the theologian Berengar of Tours in the eleventh century had sharpened the church's appreciation of the presence of Christ in the Eucharist and the power of the sacrifice of the Mass to unite Christians in charity. Even uneducated Christians had a profound sense that the Eucharist, in which Christ was present, body and blood, soul and divinity, was a powerful source of social cohesion.

This is not to say that the liturgy as celebrated in the Middle Ages was beyond criticism. In particular, with a strong sense of the distinct value of each offering of the eucharistic sacrifice, there was in the later Middle Ages a proliferation of "low Masses" celebrated by the priest with a single server and without any music, in which the diverse ministries of celebrant and deacon and subdeacon and cantor were all taken by the priest, turning what had been a manifestation of the church in her diversity of ministries into something of a one-man show. Clearly this made the liturgical ministry of the deacon increasingly seem an optional add-on to the liturgy, as the sacrament of holy orders became more focused on the priest and his power to consecrate the Eucharist.

At the same time, the diaconate appears to have remained through much of the Middle Ages as a distinct ministry with a clearly defined liturgical role, at least in some places. It is often said that during the Middle Ages the diaconate ceased being a genuine ministry and became simply a transitional step in the clerical *cursus honorum*, the final stop before reaching the pinnacle of the priesthood, and one that candidates moved through as quickly as possible. "Deacons," it is claimed, were typically priests who vested as deacons and fulfilled their liturgical function, and not men who were deacons as a permanent state. While this did eventually become the case and remained the case until the Second Vatican Council, we should be cautious about accepting this picture too quickly as a general truth concerning the diaconate in the Middle Ages. Even apart from well-known cases such as Alcuin of York in the eighth century and Francis of Assisi in the thirteenth, who were ordained to the diaconate and remained deacons their entire lives, papal records of taxes on clergy from thirteenth-century Italy indicate that almost all churches in that region had at least one deacon and one subdeacon.[50] It is unlikely that that many clergy were simply "transitioning" through these orders on their way to the priesthood. At least in some places at some times, therefore, the "deacons" of the liturgy were actual deacons.

With regard to the actual liturgical duties of the deacon, many Western medieval descriptions simply repeat what was found in a late seventh-century work called the *Epistola ad Leudefredum*, falsely ascribed to Isidore of Seville.[51] It identifies the deacon as one who assists the priest in everything associated with the sacraments, including the chrism at baptism, placing the offerings of bread and wine on the altar and also "vesting" the altar (perhaps spreading the corporal?), carrying the cross (perhaps a reference to the Good Friday liturgy?), proclaiming the Gospel and epistle, leading the prayers and the "recitation of names" (i.e., the prayer of the faithful), exhorting the attention of the assembly, and "calling out and announcing peace."[52] Even though some aspects of the liturgy had changed—notably the disappearance of the prayer of the faithful—this description was still deemed suitable some six centuries later. Similarly, other later medieval writers note the role of the deacon in ministering the chalice to the people,[53] even though by the thirteenth century the practice of the laity receiving in one kind only was nearly universal.

With regard to liturgical roles outside of Mass, we have evidence that deacons continued to perform baptisms in nonemergency situations. A thirteenth-century fresco from the baptistery in Parma shows a deacon in alb and stole baptizing an infant in the same font in which a bishop is baptizing a king, a visual representation of the statement from *De Septem Ordinibus Ecclesiae*, which I quoted above, that a person baptized by a bishop is no more holy than a person baptized by a deacon.[54] With regard to marriages, the church in the West developed a theology of matrimony that focused on the mutual consent of the couple as the essence of the sacrament, meaning that the ordained cleric present served as witness rather than the minister of the sacrament. It is not clear how often deacons served in that role of witness, though the canon lawyer Gratian mentions a case where a deacon, along with a priest, is identified as having been witness to a couple's vows.[55] At the same time, the increasing insistence that couples receive a priestly blessing as part of their wedding, and that the wedding be followed by a nuptial Mass, probably led to weddings most often being officiated by priests.

The Middle Ages continued the liturgical functions of deacons inherited from the early church. Despite the persistence of the diaconate as a distinct order into the thirteenth century, there does seem to have been gradual erosion of the order of deacons as more and more emphasis was placed on priesthood as the paradigm of ordained ministry. By the beginning of the sixteenth century there does appear to be a complete reduction of the diaconate to a brief stop on the way through the *cursus honorum* to priesthood and to a liturgical role fulfilled more often than not by priests dressed as deacons.

Deacons in the Liturgy from the Reformation to Vatican II and Beyond

The Protestant reformers tended to reject the medieval structure of orders and along with it the diaconate as an ordained ministry, substituting instead a single ordained ministry of word and sacrament.[56] In part as a reaction to this, the Council of Trent (1545–63) reaffirmed the role of the diaconate, and even decreed that diaconal ministry, as well as the ministries of the "minor orders" (doorkeeper, lector, exorcist, acolyte, subdeacon), were "only to be exercised by those holding the appropriate orders," and that these functions should be restored in churches, "as far as can be reasonably done."[57] Yet this did not happen, and it failed to happen in part because of the teachings of the Council of Trent itself.

As in the late Middle Ages, the council focused on the priesthood in its teachings on ordination and saw other ministries as instituted "to give official assistance to priests." It also reaffirmed the notion that men should "ascend through the minor to the major orders."[58] Moreover, Trent's concern to reform the education of clerics through the founding of seminaries,[59] while in many ways improving the quality of the clergy, also tended to keep those ordained to the diaconate behind the walls of the seminary as they moved with all deliberate speed toward the priesthood.[60]

Even the "liturgical deacon"—that is, the priest who, by virtue of his earlier ordination to the diaconate, vested as a deacon (or subdeacon) and fulfilled his role at a Solemn Mass—became increasingly rare. Many of the new religious orders that emerged in the sixteenth and seventeenth centuries were strongly apostolic in their focus and not much interested in elaborate liturgies, preferring the simple Low Mass celebrated by a priest and a single server.[61] Even on those occasions when a more solemn form of Mass was celebrated, this was often a *Missa Cantata* (Sung Mass), which was a sung form of Low Mass, with the tasks of the deacon and subdeacon divided between the celebrating priest and the servers. Thus even the echo of the deacon's liturgical ministry preserved in the Solemn Mass was not experienced by most people except on rare occasions. This was the state of affairs for several centuries.

When in the mid-twentieth century theologians and others began discussing the possibility of reviving the diaconate as a permanent ordained ministry, the liturgical functions of deacons—specifically their ability to solemnly baptize and to distribute Holy Communion, as well as their being bound to the recitation of the Liturgy of the Hours—were often seen as one of the things that distinguished them from laypeople who might engage in charitable, catechetical, and administrative tasks on behalf of the church. At the same time, these same theologians emphasized that the diaconate was not *simply* a liturgical ministry, but rather that the liturgical ministry was an expression of a deeper diaconal identity.[62] If the diaconate was merely a liturgical role, why should priests not fulfill it? If it was simply charitable and catechetical activities, why should the laity not fulfill it? What was needed was a recovery of a sense of diaconal ministry that encompasses the liturgical, the catechetical, and the charitable, a ministry to which one could devote oneself as a permanent vocation.

This interest in restoring the diaconate often went along with an interest in restoring and renewing the liturgy itself, often referred to as "the liturgical movement." Beginning in the early twentieth century, there was a desire to return to the ideal of Christian worship as found in the early church, in which the liturgy was a "public work" in which all of God's people took their part. The point of this, as the liturgical scholar Josef Jungmann noted, was not simply to return to the past, but so that "in the celebration of the Christian mysteries the inner wealth of the Church comes to light as of old and the children of the

Church constantly renew their joy and gladness because of their possessions and their blessings."[63] This end was sought through restoring to the laity their voice in worship through singing and speaking the responses and encouraging them to follow the action of the liturgy itself rather than engaging in their own devotions, for which the liturgy merely formed a backdrop. It was also sought through a return to the ideal of the Solemn Mass, in which the church in its diversity was manifested through a diversity of liturgical ministries.

At the Second Vatican Council (1962–65), the hopes of both those who sought a revival of the diaconate and those who sought reform of the liturgy were fulfilled. The Dogmatic Constitution on the Church stated, "it will be possible in the future to restore the diaconate as a proper and permanent rank of the hierarchy" and "to confer this diaconal order even upon married men, provided they be of more mature age." Though the diaconate was defined as a "ministry of the liturgy, the word, and of charity," the Constitution's enumeration of the deacon's duties was almost entirely liturgical:

> to administer Baptism solemnly, to reserve and distribute the Eucharist, to assist at and to bless marriages in the name of the church, to take Viaticum to the dying, to read the sacred scripture to the faithful, to instruct and exhort the people, to preside over the worship and the prayer of the faithful, to administer sacramentals, and to officiate at funeral and burial services. (*Lumen Gentium* 29)[64]

The Decree on the Church's Missionary Activity, in contrast, when discussing the restored diaconate, scarcely mentioned liturgy at all, focusing instead on the ministries of preaching, administration, and charity. The only allusion to liturgy was the statement that laypeople already engaged in these ministries would, by ordination, be "more closely bound to the altar" (*Ad Gentes* 16).

At least in North America and Europe the revival of the diaconate has been a great success, with some dioceses having almost as many permanent deacons as they do priests. Yet the tension between *Lumen Gentium* and *Ad Gentes* represents in some ways a continuing tension in the postconciliar period regarding the nature of the diaconate, and in particular the liturgical ministry of deacons. Certainly the most visible ministry of most deacons is liturgical. If you asked most Catholics what deacons do, they would probably mention reading the gospel at Mass or, perhaps, performing baptisms or officiating at weddings.

Because of this, many have criticized the restored permanent diaconate as simply being a cadre of glorified altar servers. This charge is, of course, unfair in light of the many hours spent by deacons on non-liturgical ministry. But even more importantly, the basic assumption of such a charge, that liturgical ministry is not "real" *diakonia*, should also not go unchallenged. Our survey of the history of the liturgical ministry of deacons has shown that the liturgy is the place in which the nature of the church achieves ritual expression, and that the diversity of ministries in the liturgy says something about what the church is. The prominence of the deacon's servant ministry in the public work of the liturgy points to the importance of the *diakonia* of the church as a whole as it stands before God in the act of worship.

CHAPTER 2

Building Blocks of Liturgical Ministry

In certain quarters of the church one sometimes hears that the key to well-done liturgy is simply to "say the black and do the red," by which is meant, simply say the word (the black) and follow the rubrics (the red). Like most pithy sayings and simple solutions, this contains some truth, but not the whole truth. It is certainly important to follow the words and the actions that are laid down by the church in her liturgical books. But it is entirely possible that one might read every word as written and perform every action as prescribed and the liturgy still ends up being tedious or clumsy or off-putting. This is often because the fundamental building blocks of liturgy—what it means to serve or preside, how to speak and sing and move, the role of signs and symbols—are not well understood. In this chapter I will present some of those basic building blocks so that deacons can move beyond simply saying the black and doing the red to helping God's people worship in Spirit and in truth.

Ritual and Sign

Liturgy is ritual action, in the sense that it follows a repeated pattern that is received from a normative tradition. Like other rituals both sacred and secular, it serves as a means of shaping the identity of individuals and of binding those individuals into a community: in pledging allegiance to the flag or participating in the "wave" at a sporting event, we hand ourselves over to a collective identity larger than ourselves, even as those collectivities are themselves constituted by our ritual actions. More powerfully than any idea or concept (like "America" or "The Orioles"), rituals make us who we are by shaping our emotions and affections; rooted in our bodily, animal nature, rituals operate on the level of habit-formation and muscle-memory. Formed by years of repetition, we make the sign of the cross instinctively in a moment of crisis; we fold our hands and close our eyes to place ourselves in a disposition to pray; we say "Amen" whenever we hear "through Christ our Lord." We believe, of course, that more is at work in the liturgy than simply human psychology and physiology; we believe that God is at work. But God is working *through* the power of ritual as a human phenomenon, as something suited to our natures as embodied beings. What Thomas Aquinas said of sacraments is true of all Christian ritual: "the condition of human nature . . . is such that it has to be led by bodily and perceptible things to spiritual and intellectual things. . . . And therefore divine wisdom fittingly provides human beings with aids to salvation in the shape of bodily and perceptible signs."[1] In liturgical ritual, God stoops down to engage us as the embodied animals that we are.

But human beings are particular sorts of animals: we are thinking, language-using animals. As such, liturgy is more than simply a matter of physical habituation through repetition. As Christians, we believe that our liturgy is the work of the *Logos* (i.e., word/reason/discourse) who became flesh. Liturgical ritual is therefore communicative: it conveys realities to us that are not only inscribed in the flesh but also grasped by the mind. To speak of liturgy as an ensemble of "signs" or "symbols" is one way of getting at this. Like a language, liturgy communicates through meaningful signs, and what those signs mean is expressed in our language. This is one reason why Christian liturgy is typically a matter of both words and actions. We do not simply wash someone in water; we announce the meaning of that action in saying that we are baptizing him or her in the name of the Holy Trinity. We do not simply eat bread and drink wine; we do so in the context of words of thanksgiving, remembrance, and petition. In Christian ritual, the *Logos* continues to make himself flesh, so that he can inform the hearts and minds of us who are creatures of flesh.

So when engaged in liturgical action, particularly when serving or presiding, every word and gesture matters because every word and gesture is part of a meaningful ensemble. And this meaning is not one that we who perform the ritual action get to make up willy-nilly, but rather is handed on to us by Christ through the tradition of the church. This should not engender neurotic anxiety in those who are responsible for the liturgy, however, because ultimately it is God's Holy Spirit, and not we, who is in charge of the liturgy. Therefore, having prepared for the liturgy as best as we can, we eventually have to relinquish control and let God guide the assembly to worship in Spirit and in truth.

Serving

As we have seen, one of the persistent themes in the tradition is the deacon's important but subordinate role in the liturgy. Of course, to describe it as "subordinate" is simply to say that it is "ordered" or oriented toward a higher goal—in this case, the worship of the assembly under the leadership of the presider, which itself is subordinate to a yet higher goal: the glorification of God. The subordinate role of the deacon means that he is at the service of the presider and the assembly as they put themselves at the service of God. This does not preclude the deacon exercising a certain authority within the liturgy, but it is typically more the authority of the stage manager than the principal player in the drama. The deacon gives direction to the assembly—"Let us offer each other the sign of peace," "Bow down for the blessing," "Go in peace"—but always with an eye to fostering their active participation in the liturgy. The deacon assists the presider, but always in a manner that shows that he knows when to stand out (e.g., when reading the gospel or leading the prayer of the faithful) and when to become transparent (e.g., when fetching a forgotten purificator from the sacristy or helping the celebrant find the proper page in the Missal).

There are numerous small ways in which the deacon distinguishes his servant role from a presiding role. For example, while the priest or bishop extends his hands when greeting the people with "The Lord be with you," the deacon keeps his hands joined at the greeting before the gospel reading. Though concelebrating priests always join the principal celebrant in praying the Our Father in the *orans* position—hands extended and raised—the deacon should adopt the same posture as the members of the assembly. Likewise, the deacon should not receive Communion along with the concelebrants, but afterwards, as the first of the ministers to receive. In these and other ways, the essentially ministerial role of the deacon in the liturgy manifests itself.

As the liturgy's principal servant, the deacon needs to cultivate a keen sense of "situational awareness," knowing at all times who should be doing what—whether this be the presider, readers, altar servers, or extraordinary ministers of Holy Communion—and helping them to do what they are supposed to without appearing in any way to usurp their ministries. As Aidan Kavanagh put it,

> All the lesser ministries flow from and assist [the deacon's] ministry, discovering themselves in his as their source, paradigm, and coordinator. He should therefore be able to perform all of them at least as well as anyone else, which implies that he is server of servers, cantor of cantors, reader of readers. He is butler in God's house, *major domo* of its banquet, master of its ceremonies.[2]

Indeed, though the "master of ceremonies" at an episcopal liturgy is often not a deacon, the description of that ministry found in the *Ceremonial of Bishops* offers counsel that is relevant to the deacon's role in any liturgy, noting that "during the celebration he should exercise the greatest discretion" and "carry out his responsibilities with reverence, patience, and careful attention" (35).[3]

As I said at the outset, in order to serve well, the deacon must develop an expertise not only in rubrics, but also in the theology of the liturgy. It is not enough to know *what* is supposed to happen; the deacon will serve best if he knows *why* the liturgy unfolds in the way it does. This is particularly the case with the liturgy as reformed after the Second Vatican Council, which is by design relatively flexible and adaptable to a variety of situations. For this reason, it is helpful if the deacon has a hand in planning any special liturgies (e.g., the Triduum, a visit by the bishop, a Corpus Christi procession), so that he can both bring his liturgical expertise to the planning and be sufficiently informed to make such celebrations unfold smoothly, in order that the presider and the assembly can focus on the mystery being celebrated and not on the mechanics of the celebration.

Presiding

In some contexts the deacon *is* the presider at the liturgy. This is particularly the case with baptisms and funerals celebrated outside of Mass, wedding ceremonies, and the Liturgy of the Hours. Much could be (and has been) said about how to develop skill at presiding at liturgy. Deacons are often at a disadvantage, since their liturgical presidency is typically the exception rather than the rule, and they may be less comfortable presiding than they are in a ministerial role. Of course, much that can be said about serving in the liturgy applies to presiding as well—indeed, liturgical presidency is a kind of service, and the presider ought to avoid being unnecessarily obtrusive as much as the deacon should. But there are a few further bits of advice that might prove helpful for the deacon who is presiding.

First, *know the rite you are celebrating inside and out*. Of course, this is true if one is serving as well, but when a deacon presides he rarely will have a well-trained deacon assisting him who can steer him back on track should he wander off the liturgical path. Nothing generates a sense of unease and distraction in a liturgical assembly like a presider who is fumbling pages in the ritual book looking for his place. Perhaps even more importantly, the deacon who is confident in his knowledge of the rite will be confident in leading others through it into the mystery being celebrated, which is the real role of the presider.

Second, *stick to the text and do not strive for spontaneity*. This is the element of truth in the maxim "say the black and do the red." This is related to our first bit of advice, since the need to interject comments into the rite is often a sign that the presider has not yet made the rite his own, does not feel that its words and actions are truly his words and actions. The presider should follow the text as written, except in those places where the rite allows for adaptation. Off-the-cuff deviations from the text often degenerate into grammatically confused excursions into the land of didacticism.[4] In those cases where the presider is allowed to adapt the text, the adaptation should be carefully thought out (and even written out) beforehand. Liturgies are ritual occasions, and ritual works by conforming our thoughts and feelings to itself, not by becoming the vehicle for our own personal self-expression. While we may think that our verbal alterations are making things more meaningful or authentic for the assembly, we may in fact be robbing them of a particularly beloved turn of phrase that is theirs by right. At the same time, one must avoid coming across as stiff or robotic or, worst of all, uninterested in what one is doing. To the degree that the presider has let the rite shape his own thoughts and feelings, the ritual will seem natural and not stiff or forced. Indeed, it will convey the positive values of spontaneity (authenticity, honesty) without the potential negative values (calling attention to oneself, over-personalizing a ritual that belongs to the whole church).

Third, *avoid the temptation to overexplain the ritual*. I recall an Easter Vigil that I attended at which, before lighting the paschal candle from the new fire, the priest said, "I will now light the paschal candle, which represents the risen Christ." Whereupon he lit the candle and sang "The light of Christ!" I think it safe to say that the action itself of lighting the candle and chanting the acclamation of Christ as light could have conveyed the meaning of the ritual as well—indeed, better—than the priest's explanation. A ritual carries with it a multiplicity of meanings, but these many avenues of meaning can be closed off by a presider who imposes a particular explanation on a ritual action. Yet sometimes a well-placed explanation of a rite, particularly in the case of assemblies that may be unfamiliar with Catholic liturgy (which happens frequently at funerals and weddings, and slightly less frequently at baptisms), can help to draw people into the ritual. But one needs to be careful not to overdo matters. For example, the rite baptism already incorporates "explanatory" remarks regarding the chrism, the white garments, and the lighted candle; if any further explanation of these symbols is needed, this could occur during a baptismal preparation session or perhaps be incorporated into the homily, rather than turning the entire rite into an extended catechetical or homiletic exercise.

Moving

Because a liturgy is a ritual, it involves both words and actions. *The General Instruction of the Roman Missal* states,

> The gestures and bodily posture of both the Priest, the Deacon, and the ministers, and also of the people, must be conducive to making the entire celebration resplendent with beauty and noble simplicity, to making clear the true and full meaning of its different parts, and to fostering the participation of all. (42)

Therefore, it is important for the deacon to pay attention to how he moves and gestures during the liturgy. The deacon's movement from place to place sometimes needs to be highly visible, as when he is processing with the Book of the Gospels, and sometimes needs to be as invisible as possible, as when he is going to get the presider a glass of water. If the deacon understands the liturgy it will be obvious to him which is which. He should move at a purposeful pace, neither with undue haste nor with exaggerated solemnity, conscious of the nature of the liturgical action at that point. The entrance procession, for example, is itself a ritual act and should occur at a slower pace than, say, moving from the altar to the place where he will be distributing Communion. There is no point, however, where the deacon's movement should be casual.

When moving from place to place, unless he is carrying something, he should have his hands joined in front of him and not have his arms swinging at his side.[5] Following from the principle that the deacon should not call undue attention to himself, he should take his cue from the presider as to whether he does this by placing his palms flat together (traditional in the preconciliar liturgy) or folded together. Likewise with other movements, such as bowing or striking the breast during the *Confiteor*, he should let the presider set the example: if the presider simply bows his head during the Creed the deacon should not bow from the waist, as if to display his greater piety or superior knowledge of what a "profound bow" is. Even if the deacon is convinced his way of making a particular liturgical gesture is better, this is a subject for discussion with the presider outside of the liturgy, not something to be demonstrated in the liturgy.

What constitutes appropriate movement and gesture will also depend on the scale of the space in which those movements and gestures take place. A vast cathedral will demand larger gestures and more solemn movement than a small chapel, not unlike the way in which the degree of vocal amplification needed (if any) will depend on the size of the building. While one should never minimize liturgical gestures, one might have to maximize them in a large space, even if at first it feels slightly unnatural. For example, the small signs of the cross made with the thumb on the forehead, lips, and breast at the announcement of the gospel need to be large enough that the assembly can see them, and this will depend on how close the members of the assembly are to the deacon.

Often the deacon will not be moving by himself and so will have to be conscious of the overall "choreography" of the liturgy. If leading the entrance procession with the Book of the Gospels, he should be careful not to leave the other ministers behind. When kissing the altar at the beginning and end of Mass, he should time it to coincide smoothly with the celebrant. If he accompanies the celebrant as he censes the altar, he needs to make sure he stays out of the celebrant's way. Such coordination is an application of the more general principle that the deacon's role is not to call attention to himself. It also shows the nature of the liturgy as an earthly manifestation of worship of the saints in heaven, which St. Augustine described as "the perfectly ordered and harmonious enjoyment of God and of one another in God."[6]

Speaking

The music historian Christopher Page writes,

> In an act of worship, silence may form like a film on water; anyone who breaks it is liable to be accused of gross irreverence, even a kind of cultic treason, unless the sound and the moment are all anticipated as part of an established ritual. By the third century, the deacons were associated with various kinds of licensed intervention during the Eucharistic assembly. They might speak to correct members of the congregation when they or their children proved disorderly; they might read a commemoration or give a summons to prayer, attentiveness or piety. All the tasks that deacons performed, both within the liturgy and without, are intelligible only in terms of a long-standing relation to the gospel as servants and messengers.[7]

Page points out that, even though we may think of our liturgies as a lot of words occasionally and briefly punctuated by silence, in fact all liturgical speech is a momentary eruption within an encompassing silence that we keep before the God who is beyond the mind's capacity to grasp and beyond speech's capacity to express. Thomas Aquinas reminds us that "we need to praise God with our lips, not indeed for his sake, but for our own sake; since by praising him our devotion is aroused towards him."[8] In speaking in the liturgy, the deacon assumes a responsibility that is, in the literal and nontrivial sense of the word, awesome. The deacon should speak every word allotted him in the liturgy with a sense of awe, because he does so not on his own authority, but because he has been called by Christ to be his herald and set apart by the church for this task.

Because most liturgical speech, even when addressed to God, is also meant to be heard by the assembly, the deacon must work to make sure he is audible.[9] If he is inclined to speak quickly, he must make a conscious effort to slow down. If he tends to drop his voice at the end of a phrase or sentence, he should attempt to keep his volume even, without lapsing into a monotone. The deacon must also have a sense of the acoustics of the building. Some churches are acoustically "dead" due to the use of sound-absorbing materials such as carpet, acoustical tile, and upholstered pews, so that a speaker, if amplified, can be heard while speaking in a fairly ordinary manner (without amplification it can be extremely difficult to make oneself heard in such spaces). Other churches are very acoustically "live," which makes them wonderful for singing, but a real challenge for speaking, so that one has to speak more slowly and with greater articulation than one ordinarily would. In either sort of space, the quality of the sound system can make a significant difference. If a deacon serves regularly in a particular place, it is wise to seek out feedback from people in the pews regarding audibility.

Deacons say different sorts of things in the liturgy and while every word should be spoken with awe, not everything should necessarily be said in the same way.[10] The first step is to reflect on who is being addressed in each act of speech: God ("O God, who by invisible power / accomplish a wondrous effect / through sacramental signs . . ."), the assembly ("Go in peace"), or perhaps an indeterminate addressee ("In the name of the Father, and of the Son, and of the Holy Spirit"). Even though a prayer addressed to God is meant to be heard by the people, to give voice to their prayer and, as Aquinas would put it, to arouse their devotion, it remains a different sort of speech-act than a direct address to the people. The prayer blessing the baptismal water should not be uttered in the same way as the question asks of the assembly when they renew their baptismal vows. While the deacon should avoid adopting a lofty "prayer voice" for the former, he should still keep in mind that it is God whom he is addressing and not the assembly, even though he is addressing God in a way that the assembly is intended to hear.

Of all the words the deacon speaks liturgically, the words of the gospel are preeminent. The gospel should be read in such a way as to give precedence to clarity and intelligibility. The Introduction to the Lectionary states, "A speaking style on the part of the readers that is audible, clear, and intelligent is the first means of transmitting the word of God properly to the congregation" (14). Obviously the deacon needs to make sure that he knows how all of the words are pronounced. Beyond this, while avoiding the temptation to be overly dramatic, the deacon must remember that he is telling a story and be attentive to the way in which vocal inflection can enhance or obscure meaning. This of course presumes that the deacon has reviewed the gospel ahead of time and has some idea of what he thinks it means. When the disciples in the storm-tossed boat awaken the sleeping Jesus, do they say, "Teacher, do you not *care* that we are perishing?" or "Teacher, do you not care that *we* are perishing?" or "Teacher, do you not care that we are *perishing*?" Where the vocal emphasis falls can yield subtle (and sometimes not-so-subtle) differences of meaning. The more familiar the deacon makes himself with the gospels, the more he internalizes their message, the more effectively he will proclaim them to the liturgical assembly.

Singing

While I would not go as far as Aidan Kavanagh and say that "a deacon who cannot sing is like a reader who cannot read,"[11] I do think that deacons and those who form them need to make a serious effort to make sure that they can sing their parts of the liturgy. However, most deacons receive no training in singing during their formation. If they are lucky, a kindly director of music at a parish placement might work with them on singing, but they are typically left on their own to seek out such help. Despite their lack of formal training, the one thing that people expect deacons to sing even if they sing nothing else—the *Exsultet* at the Easter Vigil—is probably the most challenging ministerial chant in the liturgy. Perhaps it is the residual trauma of this annual experience that keeps deacons from singing other things at other times.

Part of the problem is that when many people think of singing and liturgy, they think of singing *at* the liturgy, rather than singing the liturgy *itself*. That is, they think first of songs added to the liturgy at the beginning, at the preparation of the gifts, at Communion, and at the end, and then perhaps of the singing of other things (responsorial psalm, gospel acclamation, acclamations in the eucharistic prayer) as desirable add-ons, while the singing of most of the liturgy itself is seen as something reserved for extra-special occasions, if it is something done at all. Church documents, however, make clear that the most important elements of liturgical singing are not hymns or songs inserted into the liturgy, but the actual words of the liturgy itself.[12] It is the liturgy itself that is the church's great song of praise to God, and it is a song that often takes the form of a call-and-response between the ministers and the assembly. This means that the singing of the deacon and other ministers is intended to elicit the sung response of the assembly and thus the singing of the deacon, far from being a performance designed to entertain or delight, is in fact an act of ministry. Of course, even when spoken the liturgy praises God, but, as Isidore of Seville wrote in the seventh century, "In melodies the divine words more readily and ardently stir our minds to piety when they are sung than when they are not."[13] One might say that just as grace elevates and perfects human nature, liturgical singing elevates and perfects human language.

Though the Roman Missal provides music for every word that the deacon is assigned to proclaim aloud in the liturgy, this does not necessarily mean that everything that can be sung should be sung all the time. According to the principle of "progressive solemnity," one might sing certain elements to highlight especially solemn events, such as singing the gospel only on feasts such as Christmas or Easter. Or if the celebrant refuses to sing, it might seem odd for the deacon to sing certain parts: for example, if the priest does not sing the dialogue at the greeting of peace, a deacon who insists on singing "Let us offer each other the sign of peace" would simply be showboating. At the same time, a non-singing celebrant does not preclude all singing on the deacon's part. For example, the third form of the penitential rite or the prayer of the faithful or the dismissal at the end of Mass can all fittingly and naturally be sung by the deacon even when the priest sings nothing else.

The good news is that most of the ministerial chants given in the Roman Missal for the deacon are extremely simple, rarely requiring a vocal range of more than an octave. Indeed, they lie somewhere between speech and what we normally think of as song. They do not vary from week to week, so the deacon has ample opportunity to become comfortable with them. They can (and probably should) be sung unaccompanied, so the deacon is free to pick a range that suits his voice and there is no need in most cases to match vocal pitch to an instrument, which for many is the hardest part of singing.[14] From a musical perspective, most are so undemanding that there is no good reason for the deacon *not* to sing them if it serves the liturgy.

Perhaps the most common reason for not singing is that the deacon does not think of himself as "a singer." But deacons sing in the liturgy not because they are singers, but because they are ministers of the assembly, the members of which are called to make melody to God with their hearts in psalms, hymns, and spiritual songs (Eph 5:19). The deacon sings to call forth the song of the assembly.

Secondary Matters: Positioning, Vesting, Censing

As I noted in discussing ritual and signs, Catholic liturgy, whether it involves celebration of one of the seven sacraments or not, is "sacramental" in the broad sense of using the created things of this world to worship the uncreated God. In addition to the primary building blocks of serving and presiding, moving and gesturing, speaking and singing, there are other, secondary elements that deserve some attention, largely because if they are not attended to they can become a distraction for the presider and the assembly.

Positioning

Deacons should know their place, and the place of the deacon when serving is to the presider's right, the traditional position of one who stands ready to serve. Different church buildings will have their sanctuaries arranged in different ways, but, if at all possible, the deacon's seat should be immediately next to the presider's chair (GIRM 310). If there are two deacons serving at the liturgy, they may sit and stand on either side of the presider. In a procession, unless carrying the Book of the Gospels, the deacon should walk beside the presider; when the presider is the bishop the deacon should probably walk a little ahead or behind him, so as not to get in his way as he blesses the people as he goes by.

There are different opinions as to where the deacon should sit when he is presiding at a liturgy. Some would argue that since he is presiding he should sit in the presider's chair—that is, the same chair that the priest celebrant sits in during Mass. Others argue that in order to maintain the distinction between priest and deacon, the deacon should preside from the same chair where he would sit when serving at the Eucharist. Indeed, the Vatican's *Directory for Sunday Celebrations in the Absence of a Priest* specifies that when a deacon presides at a Sunday liturgy because a priest could not be present to celebrate the Eucharist, "he uses a chair other than the priest's as a symbol that the community awaits the presence of a priest" (38). It is not clear, however, whether this would also apply to other liturgies at which a deacon presides, such as a baptism or a wedding, in which he is not a mere "stand-in" for the absent priest. There are merits to both views: the first stressing more the function that is being fulfilled in the liturgy and the second stressing the identity of the ordained minister in his distinctive order. Some dioceses have policies with regard to this question, which the deacon should, of course, follow, whatever his own predilection. If there is no policy, the deacon can presumably do what seems most suitable to him.

Vesting

Unlike clerical attire, which is a sign of status (and which deacons may or may not wear, depending on diocesan policies), vestments are garments that liturgical ministers wear for the sake of the assembly. The ministers of the liturgy wear vestments to distinguish them in their various roles and as a sign that the liturgy is set apart as a time and place of sacred festivity.[15] The colors of the vestments also draw attention to the season of the liturgical year. The basic vestments of the deacon are the alb, a stole worn over the left shoulder and across the chest, and the dalmatic.[16] Worn well, vestments can make a deacon's own peculiar personality vanish into his role and into the festivity of the liturgy; worn poorly, in a slovenly or haphazard way, vestments can become a distraction.

It should be noted that the word "alb" comes from the Latin *alba*, meaning white, and symbolizes the white baptismal garment. Why one would choose to wear a tan or oatmeal-colored alb is anybody's guess. The dalmatic, a long-sleeved garment that usually matches the priest's vestments, can be omitted. But it should be borne in mind that the dalmatic is for the deacon the equivalent of the priest's chasuble and, like the chasuble, should not be foregone without good reason (e.g., if one is not available—an all-too-frequent situation in many sacristies).[17] The dalmatic is primarily a eucharistic vestment, though it may also be worn when the deacon assists at particularly solemn celebrations of the Liturgy of the Hours or presides at a Sunday celebration in the absence of a priest or a wedding ceremony.[18] For other rites, such as baptisms, and funeral services outside of Mass, the deacon should wear alb[19] and stole, with the possible addition of the cope—a cape-like vestment—on occasions of special festivity or solemnity.

Censing

The use of incense is found in religions around the world, and in the Psalms is associated with the prayers of the assembly rising up to God (Ps 141). As one early Christian source puts it,

> It is not that the Lord has need of incense. No, but we shall remember the incense of the ages of light where there is no hateful odor before the Lord, the God of the living, where there are hymns of praise.[20]

Incense helps Christians "remember" a day that has not yet arrived, the day on which all God's people will join together in the heavenly liturgy (Rev 8:3-5). But the symbolism of incense is not merely visual; it is also olfactory. It might be thought of as a "ritual smell" by which we are drawn into the mystery of God.

Since the liturgical reforms following the Second Vatican Council, the frequency and manner in which incense is used has varied widely in Catholic churches. Some parishes never use it and others use it every week. Most parishes fall somewhere in between, using incense as another form of "progressive solemnity" that can distinguish more important occasions in the liturgical year. Most parishes use incense often enough that the deacon needs to know what he is doing.

In its Western form, the censer or thurible is designed to be swung by the end of its chain while in procession and used with two hands when censing people or objects: one hand holding the end of the chain and the other hand holding the chain about eight or so inches from the thurible. When serving, the deacon typically holds the incense container or "boat" while the presider puts incense on the charcoal burning in the thurible, and then takes the thurible from the server and hands it to the presider. The *Ceremonial of Bishops* specifies that a profound bow is made toward the person or object that is to be incensed and that the censer should be swung three times when censing the Blessed Sacrament, a relic of the cross or an image of Christ, the gifts on the altar, the altar cross, the Book of the Gospels, the paschal candle, the presider and concelebrants, the assembly, and the body of a deceased person at a funeral; other relics and images of saints are censed with a double-swing of the thurible. The altar, which the deacon might cense during a solemn celebration of the Liturgy of the Hours, is censed with single swings as he circles the altar counterclockwise.[21]

Incense can incite strong reactions in people—and not only physical ones. Some people love it and are not satisfied until the altar disappears within clouds of incense. Others begin coughing before the charcoal in the thurible is even lighted. In order to give glory to God one need not use so much incense that people are left with streaming eyes and gasping lungs. Yet, as with any liturgical symbol, one should not be so puritanical that the sign is not allowed to speak. As with so many things in the liturgy, common sense and an overriding concern to help God's people worship should be one's guide.

CHAPTER 3

The Eucharist

We begin our examination of the specific liturgical roles of the deacon with his role in the celebration of the Eucharist, which is undoubtedly the most frequent liturgical role that most deacons will have. The centrality of the Eucharist in the liturgical ministry of the deacon is only fitting, for the Eucharist is, in the words of *The General Instruction of the Roman Missal*, "the high point both of the action by which God sanctifies the world in Christ and of the worship that the human race offers to the Father, adoring him through Christ, the Son of God, in the Holy Spirit" (GIRM 16). Rooted in Jesus' words and actions at the Last Supper, the Eucharist is both a ritual meal and a sacrifice, in which Christ is present to his people in his self-giving of himself to the Father, and includes them with him in that gift. In Holy Communion, the assembly is united both with Christ the head whom they receive and with Christ's Body the church, which gathers at the altar. The servant-ministry of the deacon in the eucharistic celebration serves as a reminder to the assembly that their worship of God ought to bear fruit in the world, and that, as the Second Vatican Council put it, "the renewal in the Eucharist of the covenant between them and the Lord draws the faithful and sets them aflame with Christ's compelling love" (*Sacrosanctum Concilium* 10).

One notable feature of the third edition of the Roman Missal, in comparison with the two editions that preceded it, is the greater precision with which it describes the role of the deacon in the Mass. This is undoubtedly a result of the growth of the diaconate since the Second

Vatican Council and the greater likelihood that a deacon will be assisting at Mass. The GIRM (171) summarizes the role of the deacon in the eucharistic liturgy:

assists the priest and remains at his side

ministers at the altar, with the chalice as well as the book

proclaims the gospel and, at the direction of the priest celebrant, may preach the homily

guides the faithful by appropriate introductions and explanations, and announces the intentions of the prayer of the faithful

helps the priest celebrant distribute Communion, and purifies and arranges the sacred vessels

as needed, fulfills the duties of other ministers himself if none of them is present

The GIRM also notes that if more than one deacon is present, they may divide up the diaconal duties (109). There are numerous ways of doing this and the diocese might have specific instructions. Speaking generally, when two deacons are present it is common to divide their roles into a "deacon of the Word" and a "deacon of the Eucharist." The former typically carries the Book of the Gospels in the procession, reads the gospel, and offers the biddings for the prayer of the faithful; the latter ministers at the altar, preparing the gifts and so forth. Other diaconal duties, such as leading the penitential rite, inviting the assembly to exchange the peace, and giving the dismissal, might be divided in different ways. What is most important is that the deacons and the celebrant know who is doing what ahead of time. In what follows, I will presume the presence of a single deacon at the liturgy.

The Introductory Rites

Prior to the beginning of Mass, the deacon should make sure that everything is prepared. While coordinating liturgical ministries or preparing vestments and vessels might not be the deacon's direct responsibility, and he should avoid giving liturgical coordinators and sacristans the impression that he doesn't trust them to do their jobs, it is a traditional role of the deacon to "prepare the sacrifice," as the ordination rite of the deacon puts it. This applies not just to preparing the altar during Mass, but to making sure that everything is ready for the celebration.

At the same time, it is also important that the deacon prepare spiritually for the celebration of Mass. Sacristies can be noisy and bustling places before a liturgy and it is easy for the deacon to pass from that bustle straight into the entrance procession without pausing to recollect himself, to ask God to help him minister well, to focus on the profound mystery whose celebration he will serve. It is equally important that those who will be ministering at the Mass take a moment and pray together. This might be a formalized prayer or set of prayers, or it may be an extempore prayer offered by the celebrant or deacon or one of the other ministers. Though this prayer is "extra-liturgical" since it doesn't form part of the eucharistic liturgy itself,[1] it is still important to the liturgy because it enables the ministers to carry out their tasks in a focused and prayerful way.

In the entrance the deacon walks beside the celebrant or, if he is carrying the Book of the Gospels, behind the other liturgical ministers (servers, lectors, etc.) and any others who might be in the procession (e.g., first communicants) and ahead of the celebrant and any concelebrants. He is to carry it "slightly elevated."[2] Presumably this means something higher than chest-height, but something less than as high above his head as he can reach. It seems reasonable that he should carry it so that the bottom of the book is just above his eyes. This makes the book visible to the assembly without the gesture being gratuitously ostentatious; it also has the practical benefit of allowing him to see where he is going.

If the deacon is carrying the Book of the Gospels, he should not bow or genuflect to the altar but immediately go up to the altar and place the book on it (GIRM 173). Some churches provide a stand to hold the book upright, so it can serve as a visual focus for the Liturgy of the Word, but since the ambo and presider's chair already provide two foci it seems unnecessary to provide a third, and there is nothing wrong with the book lying flat on the altar. If the deacon is not carrying the gospel book, he reverences the altar with a profound bow (or a genuflection, if the tabernacle with the Blessed Sacrament is in the sanctuary) along with the celebrant.[3] The deacon and celebrant then venerate the altar with a kiss (GIRM 173). In much of Anglo-Western culture, kissing objects might seem a bit odd, but it is a profound act of veneration for the altar of sacrifice upon which the memorial of Christ's paschal mystery will be enacted.

If incense is used, the deacon assists the celebrant in putting incense in the thurible and then may accompany him as he walks around the altar censing it. Some celebrants like the deacon to hold back the edge of the chasuble during the censing, others prefer that the deacon simply walk alongside, and others want the deacon nowhere near. If incense is to be used, the deacon should make sure he knows what the celebrant expects. After censing the altar, the deacon and celebrant go to their chairs.[4]

The Order of Mass says that, after the opening sign of the cross and greeting, the priest or deacon or other minister "may [*potest*] very briefly [*brevissimis*] introduce the faithful to the Mass of the day" (3). In practice, one rarely sees anyone but the celebrant do this. If, however, the priest is a visitor to the parish, this might be an occasion for the deacon, particularly if the parish is entrusted to his pastoral care, to introduce and welcome the celebrant. He should remember, however, that word *brevissimis* and not turn the introduction into a mini-homily or an extended discourse about the preceding week's events, the weather, the prospects of the local sports teams, and so on. It is probably also good to remember the word *potest*, which does not require but permits; on many occasions it may be most fitting to offer no introduction apart from the liturgical greeting.

On most Sundays and weekdays, the penitential rite follows. The third form of the penitential rite, which consists of invocations of Christ with the *Kyrie* as a response, can be led by the deacon (Order of Mass 6). This brief litany might fittingly be sung. Some dioceses require that only the samples offered in Appendix VI of the Missal be used, but most allow for local communities to compose their own. This responsibility sometimes falls to the deacon, so a few things should be borne in mind about these invocations. They are addressed to Christ, not the Father or the Spirit. They are invocations praising Christ's mercy, not petitions, and certainly not occasions for talking about ourselves and our sins (e.g., "For those times we have not listened, Lord have mercy"). While locally composed invocations might reflect the readings of the day, they do not have to, and much might be said for using the same invocations throughout a liturgical season in order to highlight it. Finally, and more generally, parishes with deacons can sometimes get stuck in a rut of always doing the third form, because "it gives the deacon something to do." Deacons should assure people that they have plenty to do, and remind them that in certain seasons or on certain occasions one of the other two options might be the better choice.

Another option for the Introductory Rites, replacing the penitential rite and the *Kyrie*, is the blessing and sprinkling of holy water. The deacon can assist the priest with the blessing by holding the container of water as it is blessed and accompanying the priest with it as he sprinkles the assembly. The rubrics of the Missal only mention the priest doing the sprinkling of the assembly, but in some large congregations deacons sometimes assist with this, so that the entire assembly can be sprinkled without unduly prolonging the liturgy.[5]

After the Gloria (when it is used), if there are no other ministers, the deacon should hold the book for the celebrant during the opening prayer.

The Liturgy of the Word

The Readings

A brief introduction to the Scripture readings is allowed before the first reading, and the deacon may do this,[6] but one must be cautious of overexplaining things and making the celebration of God's word into an overly didactic exercise. During the reading(s) before the gospel, the deacon should sit and listen attentively, and should respond to the responsorial psalm. Like all ministers, the deacon should model for the assembly how they themselves should participate in the liturgy, "a conscious, active, and full participation . . . namely in body and in mind, a participation fervent with faith, hope, and charity" (GIRM 18). If there are no other readers, the deacon should do the readings before the gospel, but this is something that should be avoided if at all possible.[7]

The gospel reading is reserved for the deacon when he is present. At ordination he is given the Book of the Gospels with these words: "Receive the Gospel of Christ, whose herald you now are. Believe what you read, teach what you believe, and practice what you teach" (Ordination of a Deacon 24). Occasionally a celebrant will want to read the gospel because he is giving the homily, but the deacon can politely but firmly point out that unlike things such as the third form of the penitential rite or the prayer of the faithful, in which the deacon is included among a list of ministers who might perform this role, *The General Instruction of the Roman Missal* is clear that the celebrant should read the gospel only when a deacon (or concelebrant) is not present. Of course, some celebrants might insist, in which case discretion is the better part of diaconal valor.

The ceremony surrounding the reading of the gospel, which is "the high point of the Liturgy of the Word" (GIRM 60), can be quite simple or rather elaborate. At its simplest, perhaps as one would find at a weekday Mass, the deacon makes a profound bow to the celebrant and asks his blessing. He should probably remain bowed to receive the blessing and he makes the sign of the cross as the celebrant does. Then, bowing to the altar, he goes to the ambo and, after greeting the people with his hands joined, announces the gospel, making a small cross with his thumb on the opening words of the text for the day in the Lectionary, and then on his forehead, lips, and breast, symbolizing his prayer that the gospel will be in his thoughts, on his lips, and in his heart. He then reads the gospel. At the end, without lifting the book, he says, "The Gospel of the Lord," after which he kisses the open book, saying silently, "Through the words of the Gospel / may our sins be wiped away."

The most common elaboration is the use of the Book of the Gospels rather than the Lectionary for the reading. Indeed, the GIRM seems to presume the use of the Book of the Gospels at a Mass with a deacon, though it does not explicitly require it. If it is not carried in procession, it might lie on the altar from the beginning of Mass. After receiving the celebrant's blessing, the deacon goes to the altar, bows, and takes up the Book of the Gospels. Whether the deacon goes behind the altar or in front of it to get the book depends on the particular design of the sanctuary. As he moves to the ambo, again with the book "slightly elevated," he does not necessarily need to travel by the shortest route. This is, after all, a procession. At the same time, the point of the procession is to get where it's going, so there is no need for elaborate detours; one commentator notes, "it should look festive, not as though they have lost their way."[8] When he gets to the ambo, it is fitting that he continue to hold the book slightly elevated until near the end of the gospel acclamation, at which point he should place the book on the ambo and open it. The reader of the previous reading should be instructed to remove the Lectionary, so as to avoid an unedifying pileup of books on the ambo. At the end, after kissing it, the deacon may return the Book of the Gospels to the credence table or some other dignified place, though something might be said for leaving the book open on the ambo during the homily, to visually make the connection between the homily and the readings.

The gospel procession may be accompanied by servers with incense and candles. The servers with candles might accompany the deacon from his chair to the altar and then to the ambo, or, particularly if the candles used are processional candles standing by the altar, they might wait for the deacon at the altar and then accompany the procession to the ambo (after all, it is the Book of the Gospels that the lights are intended to honor, not the deacon). During the reading of the gospel, they stand on either side of the ambo.

If incense is used, a server should bring the thurible and incense to the celebrant as the gospel acclamation begins. The deacon assists in this as usual. Then, after receiving his blessing from the celebrant, the deacon and the server go to the altar together, where the deacon gets the book. Once they have arrived at the ambo, the server should stand in a convenient place close by, a little behind and to one side of the deacon. After announcing the gospel, the deacon censes the book with three swings of the thurible, which he then gives back to the server. After the gospel, unless he is preaching, the deacon returns unobtrusively with the servers to their places. There is no procession back. If the bishop is present, however, he may exercise his prerogative to kiss the book instead of the deacon kissing it, in which case the deacon and the servers proceed to the bishop and the deacon presents the open book to him for his kiss.[9]

Another consideration is how singing is related to the proclamation of the gospel. At least from the time of Pope Gregory the Great (sixth century) until the reform of the liturgy after the Second Vatican Council, the deacon chanted the gospel at Masses with music. Some would argue that this was done for the sake of audibility in the time before microphones, since chanting allows one to project one's voice, and that with the advent of modern sound technology there is no longer a reason for chanting the gospel. Yet the chanting of the gospel was never merely utilitarian; it had its own chanting "tone," distinct from the tone with which the epistle was chanted, that served to distinguish and highlight the proclamation of the gospel. One might argue that singing the gospel remains a way of highlighting its importance, and some communities may wish, at least on occasion, to have the deacon chant the gospel. The Introduction to the Lectionary wisely counsels, "This singing, however, must serve to bring out the sense of the words, not obscure them" (14). If the deacon cannot confidently chant the gospel in such a way that the words are effectively communicated to the hearers, it is better to simply read it. The Lectionary also notes,

> Even if the Gospel itself is not sung, it is appropriate for the greeting *The Lord be with you*, and *A reading from the holy Gospel according to . . .* , and at the end *The Gospel of the Lord* to be sung, in order that the congregation may also sing its acclamations. This is a way both of bringing out the importance of the Gospel reading and of stirring up the faith of those who hear it." (Introduction 17)

For deacons who cannot effectively chant the text of the gospel itself, but still want to highlight it, this might be a better option.

If the deacon is preaching he, like the priest, can preach from the ambo or "another worthy place."[10] Preaching from the ambo, as the place from which the Word has been proclaimed, shows the homily's integral connection to the readings. But there may also be good logistical or cultural reasons for preaching from a different location (though trying to appear "folksy" probably does not count as a good reason).

The Profession of Faith and Prayer of the Faithful

During the profession of faith, if it is said, the deacon stands beside the celebrant. The rubrics call for a profound bow after the words "he came down from heaven" until "became man" (or the corresponding words in the Apostles' Creed). Though this bow has long been in the rubrics, it has not been done in many places. The deacon should follow the lead of the celebrant.

After the celebrant's introduction to the prayer of the faithful (also called the universal prayer, general intercessions, or bidding prayers), the deacon may announce the intentions, standing at the ambo.[11] If the deacon has a role in writing the intentions, he should bear in mind that these are addressed not to God but to the people, eliciting their prayers for the church and the world, which is one of the ways in which they exercise their baptismal priesthood. If the deacon composes the intentions, he should note carefully their description in the GIRM and consult the samples in Appendix V of the Roman Missal. The intentions should ask prayers:

For the needs of the church
For public authorities and the salvation of the whole world
For those burdened by any kind of difficulty
For the local community

Several intentions might be included under each of these headings.

The intentions themselves should be phrased carefully. They may reflect themes or use images from the readings, but their main purpose is to elicit prayer, not to didactically reinforce the homily. Shorter intentions are usually more effective than longer ones. The deacon is directing the prayer of the assembly, but he should strive not to be overly directive; he should tell the assembly *what* to pray for, and not so much *how* to pray. One way of doing this is not to overuse the "For . . . that . . . " pattern in intentions (e.g., "For the poor, that they might have their needs provided for"), in which the "that" clause tells the assembly how they ought to pray. While there might be some intentions that simply cannot be phrased in any other way, it is a worthwhile exercise to see if one can break out of this pattern. Also, while intentions can and should address specific events in the world and the church, the deacon should try to avoid petitions that are polarizing (e.g., "For the poor, that the heartless policies of the Republican Congress will not make their burden heavier").

The GIRM says that it is "normally" (*de more*) the deacon who offers the intentions,[12] and this seems to follow the ancient practice of the church. However, there is need for some discretion here. Some parishes have a group of laypeople who craft and lead these intentions and it would be pastorally unwise for a deacon to come in and simply take over this ministry. In such a situation, perhaps the deacon should rather ask to be included in their number and exercise his traditional care for these intentions by serving as a resource for the group, if need be, making sure that they know who and what needs praying for, helping them to understand the structure of the intentions, and so forth.

At papal Masses it has long been the custom to have a number of different laypeople announce the petitions in a variety of languages. In recent years, perhaps to honor both the recent custom of lay participation and the long-standing tradition of diaconal leadership, a new pattern has emerged in which a brief general invitation to prayer for each intention is given by the deacon, followed by a period of silence and then the more detailed announcement of the intention given by a layperson (in various languages), with a sung response led by the cantor. Thus, in praying for the leaders of nations, we find the following:

> [Deacon:]   Let us pray for legislators, magistrates, and rulers. [*Prayer in silence.*]
>
> [Lay leader:]   May the Lord's grace call forth leaders capable of courageously serving truth, justice and peace, without ever yielding to personal interests, dislikes, or compromise with evil.
>
> [Cantor:]   Let us pray to the Lord.
>
> [Assembly:]   Lord, hear our prayer.[13]

This pattern, which appears to be modeled on the Solemn Intercessions of the Good Friday liturgy, also incorporates silence in which the assembly can pray for the intention that has been announced and allows for a sung response by the assembly, both of which highlight the significance of the universal prayer as the prayer of all the baptized.

If the deacon announces the intentions, he should remain at the ambo until the celebrant has said the concluding prayer.

The Liturgy of the Eucharist

The Preparation of the Gifts

The preparation of the gifts (or, sometimes, the "offertory") is, as the name implies, a rite of preparation. As such, it should not take on a disproportionate weight with regard to the liturgy as a whole. This can be a danger because it consists in a fairly complex set of procedures necessary to prepare the altar, the gifts of bread and wine, and the assembly for the eucharistic prayer.

As the offertory song begins (if there is singing), the deacon goes to the altar while the priest remains at his chair. The deacon, with the assistance of the other ministers, places on the altar the corporal, the purificator(s), the chalice(s), the pall (if one is used), and the Missal.[14] The GIRM (178) notes that "it is the Deacon's place to take care of the sacred vessels" (i.e., those that will contain the Body and Blood of Christ). This would seem to mean that he, rather than a server, should be the one to place and arrange on the altar the chalice(s) and plates or ciboria that will hold the bread. If he is not already familiar with the preference of the celebrant, he should also make sure he knows how the Missal should be positioned.

If there is no procession with the gifts by members of the assembly, the deacon may simply bring the bread and wine from the credence table to the altar. If, however, the people present the bread and wine and other gifts—a practice that GIRM 73 identifies as "praise-worthy"—the deacon goes with the celebrant to receive these. The *Ceremonial of Bishops* says that it is the deacon who actually takes the bread and wine to the altar (145), which fits with the tradition of deacons being the ones who place the gifts on the altar, and therefore is presumably also the case when the celebrant is a priest. However, in practice the priest will often take one of the elements (usually the bread) to the altar and the deacon the other. The deacon is to hand the paten (plate) with the bread to the celebrant, though if the celebrant himself has taken the vessel with bread to the altar, it makes little sense for the deacon to take it from him only so he can hand it back. As the priest says the presentation prayer over the bread, the deacon prepares the chalice by pouring wine and a little water into it, saying silently the accompanying prayer, and then hands it to the priest. The GIRM notes that this preparation of the chalice might be done at the credence table, though if the gifts have been presented by the people and placed on the altar, it may seem odd to then take the wine to the credence table to prepare the chalice.

Two practical points should be noted here. First, if multiple chalices are used to facilitate the Communion of the faithful, they might either be filled beforehand or once the gifts have been placed on the altar. The former is preferable if there are many chalices and filling them at this point would prolong the preparation of the gifts; the latter is preferable if only a few chalices need filling, since it underscores the "one cup" (or at least "one decanter of wine") from which the assembly drinks. Second, the GIRM says that the deacon "pours wine and a little water into the chalice." What if there is more than one chalice? Should each have a little water put in it? The GIRM does not say and commentators seem divided on this question. Following the general principle that the preparation of the gifts is a preparatory rite and should not overshadow the eucharistic prayer, it is probably best in the interest of simplicity simply to mix water in the main chalice, so as not to call undue attention to a relatively minor part of the preparatory rites.

If incense is used, the deacon assists the celebrant with the placing of incense in the thurible and may, if the celebrant so desires, accompany him around the altar during the censing. Afterwards, the deacon censes the celebrant with three swings of the thurible, then any concelebrants, and finally the assembly, bowing first to each.[15] The censing of the assembly members after the gifts is important and should not be omitted because it symbolizes that the gifts on the altar—"fruit of the earth and work of human hands"—represent their lives and labor, that they themselves are part of the offering. In this way, the censing of the assembly is the final act of the preparation of the gifts. The assembly should stand before being censed and the deacon may have to gesture to them to do this. If the assembly is large, the deacon might cense it in sections, each section receiving three swings of the thurible. He then hands the thurible to a server.

The Eucharistic Prayer

The eucharistic prayer is the church's great hymn of thanksgiving to God the Father for the world's creation and redemption through the work of Christ and the Spirit. In this prayer, the assembly's gifts of bread and wine are consecrated and become the Body and Blood of Christ. Given his visibility at this point, the deacon should be particularly attentive and prayerful during the eucharistic prayer. "During the Eucharistic Prayer, the Deacon stands near the Priest, but slightly behind him" (GIRM 179). If there are concelebrants, he should not stand between them and the celebrant and altar.[16] If the celebrant desires it, the deacon might stand so that he can turn the pages of the Missal (though in my experience most priests prefer to do this for themselves).

If the pall covers the chalice, or if there is a ciborium with a closed lid, the deacon should uncover them before the epiclesis (i.e., the invocation of the Holy Spirit upon the gifts).[17] He is "normally" [*de more*] to kneel from the epiclesis until after the elevation of the chalice. Presumably reasons for not kneeling would be the same for the deacon as for the assembly: "ill health, . . . lack of space, the large number of people present, or for another reasonable cause" (GIRM 43). If there is more than one deacon at the altar and one of them is unable to kneel, it would make sense for all of them to remain standing. If the deacon is standing during the consecration, he should make a profound bow when the celebrant genuflects. The deacon may re-cover the chalice or ciborium after the consecration.

If there is a second deacon present, he might kneel at the front edge of the sanctuary and cense the host and the chalice as they are shown to the people (GIRM 179). If there is only one deacon, a server can do this.

In some places the custom arose of the deacon saying the introduction to the memorial acclamation—"Let us proclaim the mystery of faith"—since this appeared to be parallel to other diaconal admonitions to the assembly.[18] However, as the current translation—"The mystery of faith"—suggests, this is not an instruction to the congregation but a rather cryptic acclamation with an uncertain addressee. In any case, the rubrics make clear that this belongs to the priest and not the deacon.

The deacon stands through the remainder of the eucharistic prayer. At the concluding doxology ("Through him, and with him, and in him . . .") the deacon removes the pall from the chalice if necessary and elevates the chalice while the priest elevates the paten with the Body of Christ. The deacon should not join the celebrant (and concelebrants) in saying or singing the doxology. Only one chalice should be elevated, even if there are additional deacons or concelebrants present. The deacon ought to hold the chalice in two hands, so as not to look as if he is offering a toast. The deacon should try to coordinate his gesture with the priest's so that the chalice and paten are elevated to the same height. They should wait until after the assembly's "Amen" to replace them on the altar (GIRM 180).

The Communion Rite

The Lord's Prayer, in which we ask God to give us our daily bread and to forgive us our trespasses, begins the communion rite, which is intended to help the assembly prepare to receive Christ in the Eucharist. During the Lord's Prayer the deacon should not mimic the *orans* posture of the celebrant, unless perhaps this is a posture that the entire assembly takes.

The sign of peace is not simply a chance for the faithful to greet each other, but a profound symbolic act of, as GIRM 82 puts it, "ecclesial communion and mutual charity" that prepares the faithful for their encounter with the living Christ in communion. It is to be exchanged "in a sober manner," though there might be differences of culture or individual sensibility as to what "sobriety" looks like. After the prayer for peace and the celebrant's greeting of peace, the deacon, with his hands joined together (i.e., not with his arms spread wide) may invite the congregation to exchange the sign of peace. The Missal does not envision the deacon altering or adapting the words of this invitation (e.g., "Let us offer each other a sign of peace, joy, love, and friendship in our Lord and Savior Jesus Christ!") and, on the principle that it is not the deacon's role to call attention to himself, it is best to stick to the script.[19]

The celebrant exchanges the sign of peace first with the deacon (or the concelebrants nearest him and then the deacon), who then may offer it to other ministers who are nearby (GIRM 181, 239). Given the visibility and ritual attire of the deacon and celebrant, it is perhaps best if their exchange of peace not take the form of a handshake, backslap, or bear hug that one sometimes sees, but rather a more ritualized embrace. While one might not wish to adopt the practice of the liturgy prior to the liturgical reform, in which the celebrant gave the sign of peace to the deacon by placing his hands on his shoulders while the deacon cupped the celebrant's elbows and they bowed their heads to opposite sides (the verbal description sounds odder than it looked in practice), some way of exchanging the peace distinct from secular gestures of greeting seems appropriate for ministers in the sanctuary.

While the priest is prohibited, under normal circumstances, from leaving the sanctuary to exchange the sign of peace with other assembly members, the deacon is not explicitly forbidden from doing so. Indeed, the *Ceremonial of Bishops* notes that when heads of state are present in the assembly in their official capacity it is the role of the deacon or a concelebrant to leave the sanctuary to exchange the sign of peace with them (102). It might be appropriate for the deacon, in his role as mediator between the sanctuary and the nave, to exchange the sign of peace with members of the assembly who are close to the sanctuary. At the same time, it is highly *in*appropriate for the deacon, who is supposed to be the servant of the assembly, to hold up the celebration of the Eucharist while he travels to far corners of the nave to greet friends and family. As in all things, good sense and decorum should be the deacon's guide.

After the exchange of peace, the priest breaks the bread as the *Agnus Dei* is said or sung. This action, while essentially a preparation for the sharing of Holy Communion, also has symbolic significance: as St. Paul wrote, "The bread that we break, is it not a participation in the body of Christ? Because the loaf of bread is one, we, though many, are one body, for we all partake of the one loaf" (1 Cor 10:16b-17). If the directive of the GIRM is followed that the bread should "be fashioned in such a way that the Priest at Mass with the people is truly able to break it into parts and distribute these to at least some of the faithful" (321), then the deacon might assist the priest with the breaking.[20] Even if traditional small hosts are used for the Communion of the faithful, the deacon might still have a role in "breaking the bread" by helping the celebrant transfer them from a single large vessel into smaller vessels for distribution. The deacon or the servers should bring these additional vessels to the altar as the *Agnus Dei* begins.[21]

In some parishes the deacon would at this time go to the tabernacle and retrieve hosts consecrated at previous Masses for distribution at Communion. The church has for many decades, however, expressed a preference that the faithful receive Communion from elements consecrated at the Mass at which they are present.[22] This is because the Eucharist follows the pattern of the ancient "communion sacrifice" (e.g., Lev 3:1-17), in which those who offer receive back some portion of their offering after it has been consecrated to God, so that they may share in a sacrificial feast. To retrieve previously consecrated hosts during the breaking of the bread, and particularly to parcel them out into vessels for distribution, would clearly run counter to the symbolism of the Eucharist as a communion sacrifice. Therefore, in preparing for Mass it is important to prepare enough bread so that all present may receive Communion from what is consecrated. Of course, calculations of such things are never precise and it may prove necessary to use previously consecrated hosts on occasion. Particularly if the tabernacle is located outside the sanctuary it may be prudent to retrieve the hosts at this point, so as to avoid delays should there be need for them during Communion.

After the *Agnus Dei*, the priest says a private prayer of preparation and then genuflects. There is no private prayer prescribed for the deacon, but there is no reason that he cannot memorize one of the priest's and pray it at this time, as long as there is not something else he should be busy with. It would seem appropriate for the deacon to make a profound bow when the priest genuflects, but the rubrics do not mention this. If there are concelebrants, the deacon may at this point (or, if it is the custom, during the *Agnus Dei*) take a vessel with the consecrated bread to each of the concelebrants so that he may take a piece for himself. The deacon does this in silence, not saying "The Body of

Christ."[23] After the priest invites the people to Communion and receives Communion himself, he then gives Communion to the deacon under both species.[24] The deacon may then assist the priest in giving Communion to any extraordinary ministers of Holy Communion, who should only approach the altar at this point (GIRM 162).

If Communion is given under both species, the deacon should minister the cup (GIRM 182). Having the deacon minister the Body of Christ while leaving the cup to extraordinary ministers can reinforce the false impression that the former is somehow "more important" and therefore warrants an ordained minister. When ministering the cup, the deacon should hold up the cup and say, "The Blood of Christ" and then hand the cup to the communicant after he or she responds "Amen." After each communicant receives, he should wipe the lip of the chalice with a purificator and turn it slightly (with practice, these can be done with the same motion).[25] Likewise with the consecrated bread, should the Communion be distributed under only one species and the deacon ministers the host, the deacon holds it up as he says, "The Body of Christ," and places it in the communicant's hands or on the tongue after he or she responds "Amen." Communicants who receive in the hand should consume the Body of Christ in front of the minister, and the deacon may want to keep an eye out to make sure that this is happening.

If Communion is received by intinction, the deacon or another minister stands beside the celebrant, holding the chalice so that the celebrant may dip the host in it and place it on the communicant's tongue (GIRM 287). Communicants are not allowed to dip the host in the chalice themselves.[26] The GIRM speaks only of the priest giving Communion by intinction, though it seems probable that a deacon could also do so, assisted by another minister.

Sometimes, particularly in small gatherings, deacons and other ministers may feel moved to address communicants by name: "[Name,] the Body of Christ." While this is the norm in the Byzantine liturgy, it is not the practice of the Roman Rite. Should the minister happen to get the communicant's name wrong, this could turn the reception of Communion from an encounter with Christ into an occasion of embarrassment and confusion.

In some places it is the custom for non-communicants, both adults and children, to join the communion procession in order to receive a blessing, typically signaling this by crossing their arms across their breasts. This practice, for which there is no official provision, has engendered surprisingly vehement opinions both pro and con. Against the practice it might be argued that it is a *communion* procession, not some other sort, and so only communicants ought to participate in it. In favor of the practice it might be said that parents of small children often have a practical need to bring them along in the communion procession and it seems churlish for the minister of Communion to ignore them entirely. Other non-communicants who have been part of the worshiping assembly often feel that seeking a blessing at this point allows them to participate in the climax of the celebration while still respecting Catholic discipline regarding who can and cannot receive the Eucharist. Pope Emeritus Benedict recently wrote favorably of this practice, noting that those who approach are "asking for a blessing, which is given to them as a sign of the love of Christ and of the Church."[27] The deacon's safest course is probably to respect the custom of the particular parish. If the deacon does find himself in a position to bless non-communicants, he should simply make the sign of the cross over them, perhaps adding "May God bless you" or some other brief words.

After the Communion of the faithful, the GIRM states that the deacon "immediately and reverently consumes [at the altar] all of the Blood of Christ that remains" (182). He then takes the chalice and other vessels to the credence table where he purifies them, or he may purify them after Mass. Note the difference between *consuming* and *purifying*: the deacon consumes the remaining elements immediately and at the altar; he purifies the vessels at the credence table, either at that point or after the liturgy. He may also consume any remaining consecrated bread or put it in the tabernacle. Extraordinary ministers of Holy Communion may assist in consuming the remaining consecrated elements,[28] but are no longer permitted to purify the vessels.[29] If a number of chalices have been used, purifying them after the liturgy is probably the preferable option, so as not to unduly delay the liturgy. The GIRM presumes that if a deacon is present he, and not the priest, purifies the vessels (183). The deacon does not have the option that the celebrant does of purifying the vessels at the altar[30] but must do so at the credence.

"Purifying" the vessels involves wiping any small particles from the paten and other vessels for the bread with the purificator into the chalice (GIRM 163). The chalice is then filled with water (or water and wine), which is then consumed, after which the chalice is wiped with the purificator (GIRM 279). Presumably, as he purifies the vessels, the deacon could say quietly the same prayer that is appointed to be said by the celebrant: "What has passed our lips as food, O Lord, / may we possess in purity of heart, / that what has been given to us in time / may be our healing for eternity" (Order of Mass 137). It is good to remember that purification is a matter of ritual respect shown to the Body and Blood of Christ and does not preclude a sacristan or extraordinary minister washing the vessels thoroughly afterwards.

After consuming what remains of the consecrated elements (and purifying the vessels, if that is done at this point), the deacon returns to his seat and joins the celebrant and the assembly in a period of silent thanksgiving and/or a psalm or hymn of praise (GIRM 88). Then he stands beside the priest at either the altar or the chair for the prayer after Communion.

The Concluding Rites

Following the prayer after Communion, the deacon may make any needed announcements, "unless the Priest prefers to do this himself" (GIRM 184). This seems to imply that normally the deacon would make any announcements, which fits with the deacon's historic role as the one who has his finger on the pulse of the community and knows its needs. In actual practice, however, it is often the priest or a lector or a seemingly endless succession of parishioners who make these announcements. If the deacon is charged with making the announcements, he should make sure that they are brief.

After the celebrant greets the people, if a solemn blessing or a prayer over the people is to be used, the deacon says, "Bow down for the blessing."[31] Though the rubrics do not specify this, the members of the assembly presumably bow their heads at this point and the deacon should join them in doing so. The blessing finished, the deacon dismisses the people using one of the approved forms. On Easter Sunday and throughout the octave of Easter, as well as on Pentecost Sunday, a double alleluia is added to the dismissal (some parishes use this form of the dismissal on all of the Sundays between Easter and Pentecost, though the rubrics do not envision this). If the dismissal is sung, and the assembly knows the response, it can help the celebration end on a rousing note.

The deacon joins the priest in venerating the altar with a kiss and, after making a profound bow with the other ministers, departs. In practice, many parishes add a "recessional hymn," though this is nowhere mentioned in the liturgy itself. Particularly if a hymn of praise has been sung at the end of Communion, however, the ministers might leave to a musical postlude instead.

CHAPTER 4

Christian Initiation

In the previous chapter we have already begun looking at the role of the deacon in the liturgies of Christian initiation, since the Eucharist is the final, and repeatable, initiatory sacrament. In this chapter I will first discuss the deacon's role in the initiation of adults before turning to those occasions when deacons preside at infant baptisms. This is because adult initiation in many ways supplies the theological norm of initiation, in the sense that we typically look at adult initiation to figure out what initiation is, and then look at practices like infant baptism to see how they can be made to accord with that understanding. Similarly, understanding the liturgical dynamic of adult initiation can help us understand the analogous dynamics of infant baptism.

Unlike the Roman Missal, which particularly in the recent third edition defines with some precision the role of the deacon, the ritual books for Christian initiation are often vague on the role of the deacon, speaking generically of an "assisting minister" or assigning to the celebrant things, such as the dismissal of catechumens, that tradition would indicate should be the role of the deacon. Presumably future editions of these rites will better reflect the reality of the increasing number of deacons ministering in the church and delineate their role more clearly.

Christian Initiation of Adults

Only under extraordinary circumstances would a deacon perform the baptism of an adult, since the initiation of adults ordinarily involves the reception of confirmation and first Eucharist along with baptism within the same liturgy.[1] The most likely circumstance would be a person in danger of death. In such a case the deacon should use the rite of Christian Initiation of Adults in Exceptional Circumstances,[2] omitting the sacrament of confirmation, or, if this is not possible, the abbreviated rite of Christian Initiation of a Person in Danger of Death.[3] With either form, he should, if at all possible, give the person baptized his or her first Communion from the reserved sacrament. Another possible circumstance would be if there were a great number of adults to be baptized, in which case a deacon might baptize some while the celebrant is baptizing others.[4]

The normal role of a deacon in the initiation of adults is through his participation in the *Rite of Christian Initiation of Adults* (RCIA). Some might think that this is more fittingly treated under the heading of the deacon's ministry of the Word, rather than his liturgical ministry, since much of his involvement might be catechetical. But it is important to remember that we are here speaking of the *rite* of Christian initiation. The RCIA is not a "class" for converts, but a series of ritual events, of liturgies, that are interwoven with catechesis. These liturgies are not "graduation ceremonies" marking the various phases of the RCIA; rather, the catechesis during the RCIA serves to prepare those who will be participating in those liturgical celebrations to do so with the greatest possible spiritual fruit.[5] Given the significant role that deacons often play in the catechesis of adults, it is fitting that they take an active role in the liturgies of the catechumenate.

Before discussing the deacon's role in the catechumenal rites, I would underscore that these are rites for those who are *unbaptized* and are seeking to become Christians in the Catholic Church. The RCIA provides some analogous rites for adults who are already baptized but uncatechized and who are seeking to be received into full communion with the Catholic Church, which I shall mention where appropriate. But such people should never take part in the rites of the catechumenate itself. To have baptized adults seeking full communion participate, for example, in the Lenten scrutinies is to treat them as if they were unbaptized, which is tantamount to denying the efficacy of their baptisms and their status as Christians. The ecumenical and theological implications of such liturgical malpractice are significant.

The Rite of Acceptance into the Order of Catechumens

This is the first rite of the RCIA, by which one who has been inquiring into the Christian faith becomes a catechumen (a Greek term that means "hearer"). A catechumen has taken the first step of being incorporated into the church and has a right to be married in the church[6] as well as to receive a Catholic burial.[7]

Though the RCIA envisions this rite being celebrated in the context of the celebration of the Eucharist, if for some compelling reason it is not, a deacon might preside (48). If, as would be typically the case, the deacon does not preside, he might, particularly if he has had a role in the preceding period of inquiry, call the candidates forward by name. He should announce the intentions in the litany for the catechumens, the special intercessions of the rite that should normally be distinct from the prayer of the faithful, which follows the dismissal of the new catechumens. Though the rite presumes that it is the celebrant who dismisses the catechumens at the end of the Liturgy of the Word (RCIA 67), both the logic of the rite and historical precedent would suggest that the deacon could do this. On ordinary Sundays, if the catechumens are dismissed this would also be properly the role of the deacon.

There is a similar rite of welcoming for baptized but previously uncatechized adults, but if they and the catechumens are included in the same celebration, a strict distinction between the two groups must be observed (see RCIA 507–29).

Celebrations of the Word during the Catechumenate

One way to ensure the properly liturgical character of the RCIA is to have frequent "celebrations of the Word" for the catechumens, by which they learn the practice of liturgical prayer. Indeed, the RCIA suggests that these might be done as part of the weekly meetings for instruction, "so that these will occur in a context of prayer" (84). Particularly if he is participating in the instruction of the catechumens, it would be highly appropriate for the deacon to preside at these celebrations, though they do not require an ordained presider. The RCIA (86–89) outlines the basic structure of these celebrations:

opening song

one or more readings, "proclaimed by a baptized member of the community," along with one or more responsorial psalms

a brief homily

a concluding rite such as a minor exorcism or blessing and, at least on occasion, anointing with the oil of catechumens

Participating in such celebrations week in and week out as a prelude to their instruction, catechumens will come to think of the RCIA less as "convert classes" and more as a time of prayerful formation.

A few specific points might be noted. There is flexibility in how formal the celebrations are. In most cases, a deacon who presides will want to vest in alb and stole, though if the celebration takes place outside a sacred space the deacon may choose not to vest. Even in those cases, care should be taken to set the celebration aside as a ritual event, perhaps by the use of candles or icons. For the opening song something very simple would be appropriate, such as a Taizé or other chant that could be repeated for several weeks so as to become familiar. The Scriptures should be read by someone who is baptized (perhaps a sponsor or a catechist), since the catechumens are still "hearers" and not yet proclaimers of the word of God. The readings might be chosen to fit with the topic of instruction for that meeting and the homily could serve as a brief introduction to the instruction that is to come. Given some of our cultural associations with the term "exorcism," care should be taken to give an explanation that these are prayers directed to God that "draw the attention of the catechumens to the real nature of Christian life, the struggle between flesh and spirit, the importance of self-denial for reaching the blessedness of God's kingdom, and the unending need for God's help" (RCIA 90). The deacon says the prayer of exorcism with hands extended over the catechumens while they bow or kneel.

On occasion, catechumens can be anointed. Deacons can anoint with the oil of catechumens (98), but cannot bless the oil. It should be explained to the catechumens that the anointing "symbolizes their need for God's help and strength so that, undeterred by the bonds of the past and overcoming the opposition of the devil, they will forthrightly take the step of professing their faith and will hold fast to it unfalteringly throughout their lives" (99). When anointing occurs, it follows a prayer of exorcism, which the deacon says with hands extended over the catechumens while they bow or kneel.[8] The catechumens then stand upright and the deacon anoints them on the breast or on the hands while saying the prescribed formula (103). The anointing may be followed by a prayer of blessing, which the deacon prays with hands outstretched once again over the catechumens, possibly followed by an individual laying on of hands. A catechist who has received permission from the bishop may also perform the exorcism and blessing, but not the anointing (16, 98).

Rite of Sending/Rite of Election

The typical pattern in the United States is that on the First Sunday of Lent the rite of sending, at which parishes inscribe the names of those who will be baptized in the Book of the Elect and then send them forth for the rite of election with the bishop, is celebrated during a Mass in the morning. Then in the afternoon those who are to be baptized gather at the cathedral or some other suitable location with the bishop or his delegate for the actual rite of election, during which representatives of the parishes present the catechumens to the bishop and testify to their readiness for initiation, after which the bishop chooses or "elects" them to be among those who will receive the sacraments of initiation at the Easter Vigil. After this they are no longer catechumens, but members of the elect.

Though the rite of sending normally occurs in the context of the Sunday Eucharist, if it is celebrated outside of the Eucharist presumably a deacon could preside over the entire rite. In either case, the rite of sending occurs after the homily. The deacon, if he has been involved in the formation of the catechumens, presents them to the pastor of the parish (RCIA 111). As at the rite of welcoming, he should also announce the intentions of the intercessions for the catechumens, and it would be appropriate for him to dismiss them before the prayer of the faithful. The prayer of the faithful, as well as the profession of faith, may be omitted "for pastoral reasons."[9]

While the liturgical books seem to prefer that the celebration of the rite of election be in the context of the Eucharist (RCIA 128), in practice it most often occurs as part of a celebration of God's word. A deacon would normally read the gospel, just as at Mass, and announce the intentions in the intercessions for the elect. A deacon may also be the one to formally present the candidates for election to the bishop (130). Though the rite speaks of the celebrant dismissing those present at the end, logic and tradition would seem to indicate that this may be done by the deacon.

Baptized but previously uncatechized adults can be included in these celebrations, but care must be taken that the distinction between them and the catechumens is maintained (see RCIA 530–61).

Lenten Rites of the Catechumenate

There are two sorts of rites for catechumens that occur during Lent, which the RCIA refers to as the period of purification and enlightenment: the scrutinies and the presentations. The scrutinies are ideally celebrated on the Third, Fourth, and Fifth Sundays of Lent, with the presentation of the Creed celebrated in the week following the first scrutiny and the presentation of the Our Father celebrated in the week following the third scrutiny (RCIA 146, 148–49).

The scrutinies are "rites for self-searching and repentance" that "are meant to uncover, then heal all that is weak, defective, or sinful in the hearts of the elect; to bring out, then strengthen all that is up-right, strong, and good" (141). All three have a common form: after the homily, the elect come forward with their godparents. The deacon could fittingly signal when this is to occur by inviting them forward. After the celebrant addresses both the assembly and the elect, inviting them to silent prayer, the RCIA says that he asks them to kneel. This could also be done by the deacon, fulfilling his role as the one who gives directions. After an appreciable period of silent prayer, they stand and the deacon leads the intercessions for the elect, during which their godparents stand with the elect, placing a hand on their shoulder. The exorcism follows, which takes the form of two prayers by the celebrant, one addressed to God the Father and the other to Christ, between which the celebrant lays hands on the elect. After this the elect are dismissed, which would fittingly be done by the deacon. If for some reason the scrutinies cannot be included in the Sunday Eucharist, they might occur in the context of a celebration of God's word at which the deacon presides, in which case he may also preside over the scrutinies (145). What is key in the celebration of the scrutinies is to allow the silent prayer before the intercessions to be lengthy enough that the elect can truly open their hearts to God so as to "progress in their perception of sin and their desire for salvation" (143).

The presentations are a ritual handing over of the Creed and the Lord's Prayer as fundamental texts of Catholic Christians, "in order to enlighten the elect" (147). The RCIA envisions these taking place at a Mass during the week at which the parish community is present (157). Because the parish Mass schedule might not accommodate such a gathering, the presentations might also take place at a celebration of God's word at which a deacon presides. In both of these liturgies, the elect *receive* the words of the Creed and the Lord's Prayer; they do not recite these words themselves. The structure of the two rites is slightly different. For the presentation of the Creed, the deacon calls the elect forward after the readings and homily, and the presider invites them to listen to the words of the Creed and to "receive them with a sincere heart and be faithful to them" (160). The baptized faithful who are present then recite either the Apostles' or Nicene Creed as the elect listen. For the presentation of the Lord's Prayer, the deacon invites the elect forward before the gospel reading, which consists of Matthew's version of the Lord's Prayer. The homily follows. In both cases, the rite concludes with a prayer over the elect and their dismissal.

Also numbered among the rites celebrated during Lent are the Preparation Rites on Holy Saturday, which always occur in the context of a celebration of God's word. Some dioceses have regional celebrations of these rites, bringing together the elect from different parishes. A deacon could preside at these rites or assist as needed, for example, helping to perform the *Ephphetha* rite if there are many elect present (199).

Celebration of the Sacraments of Initiation

The duties of the deacon at the Easter Vigil will be discussed below; here I will discuss only those parts related to the sacraments of initiation.

After the homily, the deacon calls forth the candidates for baptism (219). If the font is located outside of the sanctuary, the candidates may either gather immediately at the font or go first to the sanctuary and then process to the font with the ministers, led by the paschal candle, during the singing of the litany of the saints. The deacon takes his place beside the celebrant at the end of the procession.[10] At the end of the litany the deacon might take the paschal candle and make sure that he has it ready to hand to the celebrant near the end of the blessing of the font so that he can lower it into the water. After the blessing, if the baptism is celebrated in the sanctuary, the deacon or server could return the paschal candle to its stand; otherwise, he should hand it to a server. After the candidates renounce sin and profess their faith,[11] they are baptized, preferably by immersion, but pouring water over the head is also allowed. The deacon might stand ready with towels. If infants are baptized at the Vigil, they are anointed with chrism on the top of their heads immediately after their baptism. The *Ceremonial of Bishops* states that either presbyters or deacons should perform the anointing while the bishop says the words associated with the anointing.[12] The neophytes are then clothed in a white garment by their godparents. The deacon can assist with this if need be. The deacon then hands the paschal candle to the celebrant or holds it himself as the godparents are invited forward to light the candles that they will present to the newly baptized. The RCIA assigns this invitation to the celebrant, though these sorts of invitations are more typically given by the deacon.

After the newly baptized have received their lighted candles, if baptism has been celebrated outside the sanctuary, they proceed back to the sanctuary for the sacrament of confirmation.[13] Again, the deacon walks beside the priest. During confirmation itself, the deacon may hold the container of chrism while the celebrant performs the anointing. The deacon should not join in the laying on of hands, as assisting priests do.

After the newly baptized have been confirmed, the members of the congregation renew their baptismal promises.[14] They are to hold candles, presumably lighted from the paschal candle; the deacon might assist in the lighting of these. After the renewal of promises, as the assembly is sprinkled, the neophytes (i.e., the newly baptized) are escorted to the places in the assembly (RCIA 236). The deacon can assist the celebrant with the sprinkling, but, particularly if he has had a significant role in the catechumenate, he might more fittingly take the role of leading the neophytes to their place in the assembly. If the blessing of baptismal water was not done in the font, the deacon and other ministers should "reverently carry the vessel of water to the font."[15] After this, Mass continues with the deacon leading the prayer of the faithful.

Though reception of baptized but uncatechized adults at the Easter Vigil is discouraged,[16] the United States edition of the RCIA does provide a rite for when that occurs. In this rite, the renewal of baptismal promises occurs after the giving of the lighted candle to the newly baptized and before confirmation. Those to be received remain with the rest of the assembly until after the sprinkling with baptismal water; then they are invited into the sanctuary. Though the RCIA assigns this invitation to the celebrant, it would not be inappropriate for the deacon to give this invitation, particularly if he had a significant role in their formation. After they make their profession of faith, the celebrant says the words officially receiving them into the church; though to my knowledge it is nowhere expressly forbidden for deacons to perform this act of reception, the RCIA presumes that it will be done by the bishop or presbyter who will go on to confirm the newly received (481). This occurs immediately after their reception, along with the confirmation of the newly baptized.

Postbaptismal Catechesis or Mystagogy

When baptism is celebrated at the Easter Vigil, the period of myste-gogy lasts until Pentecost, and serves as "a time for the community and the neophytes together to grow in deepening their grasp of the paschal mystery and in making it part of their lives through medita-tion on the Gospel, sharing in the eucharist, and doing the works of charity" (RCIA 244). The RCIA is somewhat vague about the liturgical component of this period of catechesis, saying, "its main setting is the so-called Masses for neophytes, that is, the Sunday Masses of the Easter season" (247). It is not clear whether these are special Masses primarily for the neophytes (though, "the entire local community should be invited to participate with them"), or simply the regular Sunday Eucharist, at which a special place in the assembly is set aside for the neophytes, and the homily and intercessions "take into account the presence and needs of the neophytes" (248). Practically speaking, since most pastors would be loath to add an additional Mass to the Sunday schedule, the latter possibility is the more likely scenario, so deacons who are preaching or announcing the intentions of the prayer of the faithful should be particularly diligent about remembering the role that these liturgies play in the period of postbaptismal catechesis.

The RCIA also says that on or around Pentecost Sunday, "some sort of celebration" should mark the end of the period of mystagogy and that "festivities in keeping with local custom may accompany the oc-casion" (249). This could take the form of Evening Prayer, at which the deacon might preside, in which all process during the *Magnificat* to the baptismal font to renew their baptismal vows, after which they are sprinkled with water from the font, and the liturgy concludes with the intercessions and closing prayer. This could be followed by a com-mon meal.

The Baptism of Children

The origins of the practice of infant baptism reach back to the earli-est years of Christianity—though how early we are not sure. It is pos-sible that within the first century infants were baptized as part of entire households who converted to Christianity (see Acts 16:33). We know that infants of Christian parents were baptized when they were in danger of death and, given the high level of infant mortality in the ancient world, it is possible that the practice spread from there. By the sixth century infant baptism was well established as the norm in Christian areas.[17] In recent decades the increasing secularization of Western society, and doubts about whether those baptized as infants would receive any formation and nurture in the faith after their baptism, have led some to question the practice, but today it remains common for Catholic parents of varying degrees of practice and of commitment to their faith to bring their children for baptism. In celebrating the sacrament of baptism it is good to remember the different levels of understanding and commitment of those present.

Though deacons rarely if ever baptize adults, they often baptize children, particularly when this is done outside of Mass. There are differences of opinion as to whether a deacon can perform the baptismal part of the liturgy when the baptism occurs in the context of the Eucharist. On the one hand, there appears to be no explicit rule prohibiting this. On the other hand, we might extrapolate a general principle from the *Book of Blessings*, which states, "whenever a priest is present, it is more fitting that the office of presiding be assigned to him and that the deacon assist by carrying out those functions proper to the diaconate."[18] This would seem to indicate that a deacon defers to a priest in taking the role of liturgical presider. But this is not stated as something absolute (i.e., "it must be the case") but rather as "more fitting." This would seem to indicate that in some circumstances a deacon *could* preside at the baptismal part of the liturgy (say, if he had a particularly close pastoral relationship with the family), but that this would be exceptional. So in what follows I will presume a baptism celebrated outside of the context of Mass, with the deacon as presider.

The Reception of the Children

Prior to the celebration the deacon should make sure that everything is prepared: the font is filled with (warm) water, the paschal candle is lighted, the oils are where they can be accessed when needed, towels and baptismal candle are ready, and so forth.

The liturgy can begin with a song. There is no reason not to make baptisms celebrated outside of Mass as festive and solemn as possible; a parish should be willing to invest musical and other resources in their celebration just as much as they would in the Sunday Eucharist. Even if parish musicians cannot be present, the deacon might lead the assembly in song at various points.[19] The rite of baptism includes a number of biblical and other texts for sung acclamations (*Rite of Baptism for Children* [RBC] 225–45), but given the occasional nature of the assemblies who gather for baptisms, familiar hymns such as "Amazing Grace" or "Now Thank We All Our God" or "Holy God, We Praise Thy Name" might work better.

The deacon, wearing an alb or surplice and a stole "of festive color" (white is traditional) and perhaps also a cope, goes to greet the parents and godparents at the entrance of the church or some other place where they are gathered (RBC 35). The rite of baptism proposes different locations within the church for the different actions of the liturgy, and it is good to make as much use as possible of the potential for movement, both for its symbolic value as well as to keep the participants (who often include families with younger children) engaged. If possible, one might have all who are present join in moving around the church.[20] Beginning at the entrance to the church has the obvious symbolism of baptism as an entry into the worshiping community.

The deacon greets all present, perhaps with a formal liturgical greeting (e.g., "The Lord be with you"), though the rite seems to presume something less formal, since it says that in this greeting the presider is to remind them briefly "of the joy with which the parents welcomed their children as gifts from God, the source of life, who now wishes to bestow his own life on these little ones" (RBC 36). The deacon should remember that this greeting is to be *brief*—this is not the time for a homily. The deacon then asks what name the parents have given the child and what it is that they are asking of God's church for their child. It might be good before the liturgy begins to remind the parents of what their answer to the second question is (i.e., "baptism"—presumably they know the answer to the first question already). He then asks about their readiness to undertake their duties as Christian parents. If there are many children to be baptized, the second and third questions may be addressed to the entire group of parents and answered by them together, though if at all possible it would be better for each family to answer separately.

After asking the godparents as a group about their willingness to assist the parents, the celebrant signs each child on the forehead with the sign of the cross and invites the parents and, if desired, the godparents to do so as well. Experience indicates that there is almost no way to keep this moment from being slightly chaotic, as children are passed around and touched by multiple people. The best policy is to keep in mind that we are dealing with babies here and that God is not disturbed by a little bit of noise (indeed, one might suspect that God delights in it). As Pope Francis said in a homily at Mass on the feast of the Baptism of the Lord, during which he baptized a number of babies, "Today the choir sings, but the most beautiful choir is the children making noise . . . Some of them will cry, because they are uncomfortable or because they are hungry: if they are hungry, mothers, feed them with ease, because they are the most important ones here."[21]

Celebration of God's Word

At this point, the deacon, parents, godparents, and even the whole assembly, can move to the location of the Liturgy of the Word. There can be singing during this procession. It is permitted to take the children out at this point, but since they have just been welcomed into the Christian assembly, it would seem a poor sign to now remove them.

At a minimum, the Liturgy of the Word consists of a reading from one of the gospels, though other readings and a responsorial psalm can also be included (RBC 44). If readings in addition to the gospel are used, it would be appropriate to have these read by one of the laypeople present. Do not ask someone on the spur of the moment to do this, but arrange it in advance so that the readings can be prepared and proclaimed effectively. If a responsorial psalm is used, it is ideally sung.

There is no indication that the gospel reading is to be accompanied by the ritual actions used at Mass to solemnize the proclamation of the gospel: the assembly standing, the greeting of the assembly, and their responses before and after the reading. Indeed, the option of having two readings from the gospels (RBC 44) raises questions of how one would fit two readings into one solemn proclamation of the gospel. At the same time, the rite does provide verses for the gospel acclamation, which would suggest that the gospel is to be read just as it would be at Mass (198–203). In the end, this is a place where the deacon should exercise his own judgment. Particularly if other readings are used, such that the celebration of God's word closely resembles the Liturgy of the Word at Mass, then it would seem to make sense to read the gospel just as one would at Mass. If, however, only a reading from a gospel is used then it might be better to read it without any special ceremony.

The homily can be brief, so as not to strain the patience of the babies or their no doubt distracted parents. This might be focused on the readings, but it might also appropriately unfold some of the symbolic richness of the rite itself: the oils, the water, the sign of the cross, the lighted candle, and so forth. Again, the deacon should be aware of the level of understanding of those present and tailor his words to their needs. For some, the most basic truths of the Christian faith might need to be explained: that God created us and loves us and wants to share his life with us through Jesus and the Spirit. For others, a deeper meditation on baptism, the paschal mystery, and life in the Spirit might be appropriate. Of course the challenge to preaching at a baptism (and weddings pose similar challenges) is that often those present will represent a broad spectrum of engagement with the Christian faith.

After the homily, the deacon should ask all present to pray for a moment in silence, after which there might be a song (RBC 46). The intercessions follow, for which five forms are provided, but with the note that "petitions may be added or omitted at will, taking into consideration the special circumstances of each family" (216–20). Only the fourth form has a verbal clue to elicit the peoples' response (i.e., "We pray to the Lord"); it might be advisable to add this to the other prayers so that those present know when to make their response. Like the prayer of the faithful at the Eucharist, the presider (in this case the deacon) introduces the intercessions, and then a "leader" reads the petitions. Unlike the prayer of the faithful, however, the petitions are not directed to the assembly, asking their prayers for specific things, but rather are directed to God. A member of the assembly might read the petitions, if there is someone who is prepared in advance to do so. As with the Scripture readings, it might be better for the deacon to do this himself than to draft someone at the last minute.

The intercessions conclude with a brief invocation of the saints. If the children have been taken to a place apart they are now brought back. The rite says that the celebrant "invites all present to invoke the saints," but it provides no model text for such an invitation. The deacon should think this through beforehand and make sure that the invitation is concise. The patron saints of those being baptized should be added to the saints provided, as well as the patron of the parish and other saints who are of particular significance to the families (RBC 48). The litany could be sung, led by the deacon or a cantor.

The invocation of the saints leads into the prayer of exorcism, for which two options are given, and the anointing with the oil of catechumens. Neither of the prayers is an exorcism in the sense of directly addressing and commanding the devil (as was the case in the rite before the Vatican II reforms) but rather are prayers directed to God to free the child from the power of evil. In the United States the anointing can be omitted "when the minister of baptism judges the omission to be pastorally necessary or desirable" (RBC 51). This is an ancient element in the liturgy of baptism in both East and West—symbolizing the ancient practice of the soldier or athlete rubbing himself with oil before entering into combat or competition—and should not be omitted lightly. If it is omitted, the deacon is to lay his hand on those to be baptized after saying the appointed text. The anointing is done on the chest and parents should be warned in advance to make sure that the child's clothes are loose enough to allow access. As with all signs, the amount of oil used should not be stingy.

Celebration of the Sacrament

The deacon now moves with the children and their parents and godparents to the font. If the font is not near where the assembly has gathered for the celebration of God's word, the entire assembly should move with them so that it can see the baptism. A song can be sung during this procession (RBC 52).

The deacon then blesses the water in the font. He should, if possible, pray with his hands extended, which might require him to get someone to hold the ritual book for him. He touches the water or makes the sign of the cross with his right hand at the point indicated in the prayer, but does not lower the paschal candle into the water, as is done at the solemn blessing of the font at the Easter Vigil.[22] Three forms are provided for this (54). The first form, which is also used to bless the font at the Easter Vigil, includes a much fuller account of the role of water in the history of salvation and would be appropriate for baptisms at which those in attendance have a deep appreciation of the Christian faith. This prayer can be sung to the chant that is found in the Missal.[23] The second and third forms are shorter and incorporate congregational responses and so might prove more engaging to an assembly that includes some who would miss the first prayer's allusions to Noah, the exodus, and so forth. The deacon will have to inform those present of what the responses are within these prayers and find some way to prompt them to make it. These prayers also provide an alternate text for use if the water is already blessed (as may be the case during Easter season). If the font is not designed, as some modern fonts are, so that water is continuously flowing through it, the deacon could have someone slowly pour water from a pitcher into the font during the prayer of blessing, to signify that the water of baptism is "living" water.

After blessing the water, the deacon addresses the parents and godparents concerning their duties and asks them to reject sin and profess their faith. The rite specifies that the questions that follow are addressed to the parents and godparents, not the assembly, so presumably only the parents and godparents would answer them.[24] Two forms of the renunciation of sin are provided, the first of which is more ancient and the second of which is a bit more expansive. The presider's statement at the end of the profession of faith, "This is our faith . . ." and the congregation's "Amen" to it serves as their affirmation of the parents' and godparents' profession. This could be sung, or a suitable song could be sung instead (RBC 59).

The actual baptism should be either by threefold immersion or pouring ("infusion"). If there are multiple children being baptized in the same service, the same mode of baptism should be done for all, unless there is a compelling reason otherwise. Immersion presumably means actually submerging the child in the water; while this is identified as "more suitable as a symbol of participation in the death and resurrection of Christ,"[25] and is the norm in the Christian East for all baptisms, it is rarely seen in the Roman Rite for the baptism of infants. More often one sees pouring while the child's head is held over the font, or something of a hybrid of immersion and pouring, in which the lower part of the child is submerged in the font and water is poured over its head and upper body. This seems quite a fitting sign, since baptism is a ritual bath and this is the way in which parents typically bathe their children.[26] This of course presumes a font of sufficiently generous size that an infant can fit into. Also, if the child is either immersed or placed into the font, it will need to be undressed at some point. This might be done at the time of the first anointing, with the child then being wrapped in an absorbent towel until right before the baptism.

If water is poured over the head only, the mother and/or the father should hold the child face up while the deacon pours water over the forehead, trying to avoid having the water run over the baby's face. If the child is placed in the font to have water poured over it, the father and/or the mother should hold the child in the water while the deacon pours water over the head and upper body.[27] Some deacons prefer to use a small pitcher or baptismal shell for pouring while others prefer to use their cupped hands. In either case the amount of water used should be generous. The deacon must both pour the water and pronounce the baptismal formula. This should not be divided between two different people since the action and the words together constitute the sacramental sign. Godparents might stand ready with a towel to dry the child's head or body. At the end of each baptism, the congregation may sing an acclamation. The Alleluia from a gospel acclamation that is familiar to them from Mass could serve this purpose well.

After all the children are baptized, the deacon anoints them with chrism in silence, after speaking the explanatory words. Note that these words are addressed to the child, not the parents and godparents, and should be spoken in such a way as to make that clear. Here especially the oil should be used lavishly, because it represents the admission of the newly baptized into Christ's messianic roles as priest, prophet, and king (remember that "messiah" means "anointed one"). The deacon anoints the top of the child's head (the bishop will later anoint the forehead in confirmation). There is no need to wipe away the oil afterwards; parents sometimes comment that the smell of the chrism on their child's head reminds them of the baptism for days afterward.

The words at the giving of the white garment are likewise addressed to the child. If the child gets completely wet during baptism, it is best that he or she be dressed in other clothes for the first part of the liturgy and then clothed in the white garment after the anointing with chrism. This might take a bit of time, but one should remember that the dressing of the child is itself a ritual action and need not be thought of as somehow "holding up" the real ritual. If water is poured only over the head of the child, then the usual practice is for the child to be dressed in its white garment from the outset of the liturgy. In that case, the deacon should touch the garment as he says the words, "See in this white garment . . ." In some places a white bib or mini-stole is placed on the child at this point. This is probably less than ideal, since it does not so clearly represent the enveloping character of being "clothed in Christ" that a genuine garment does. Of course, if there are volunteers in the parish who are devoted to sewing such things, one ought to think carefully about how one would move toward discontinuing their use.

The baptismal rite says that the celebrant "takes the Easter candle and says: / Receive the light of Christ," after which someone (it suggests the father or godfather) lights the child's baptismal candle from it and the celebrant addresses the parents and godparents concerning their responsibilities now that the child is baptized (64). In practice, it is often awkward to remove the paschal candle from its stand and so it remains in place, with a godparent lighting the baptismal candle from it (often the godfather, simply because he is usually taller and can reach the top) and the celebrant then saying, "Receive the light of Christ." Remember that these words are addressed to the child and the words following to the parents and godparents. The deacon could also add some words suggesting that the candle be lighted for family prayers on the anniversary of the child's baptism (or this suggestion could be made in the pre-baptismal catechesis). If such a practice is encouraged, a parish might consider using baptismal candles that are substantial enough to be burned more than once. The baptismal candles should remain lighted until the end of the rite.

The *Ephphetha* rite, in which the celebrant touches the child's ears and mouth with his thumb, is a rite for catechumens that has been transformed here into a post-baptismal rite for infants, anticipating their future ability to hear and proclaim God's word. It is optional and may be omitted at the deacon's discretion. Some may feel that one more ritual at this point is simply piling on, though the ritual itself is brief.

Conclusion of the Rite

The deacon, the newly baptized, and their parents and godparents move from the font to the altar. If the font is outside the sanctuary this might take the form of a procession accompanied by song. Standing at the altar, the deacon addresses the assembly in words that look forward to the completion of Christian initiation in confirmation and the Eucharist. He invites them to join in praying the Lord's Prayer, which all recite or sing together.

The celebration concludes with a final blessing, for which four options are given (RBC 246–49). The first and third options bless the mother, then the father, and then the whole assembly. The second option blesses the children, the parents, and then the assembly. The fourth simply blesses all those present. These last two would be appropriate if either the mother or father of one or more of the children is not present. The rite directs that the mother is to hold the child as she is blessed. It would seem fitting, if there is a separate blessing for the father, that he take and hold the child as he is blessed as well.

The rite ends with the blessing. Some celebrants like to add the sign of peace, and if this is done the invitation used at Mass would be appropriate.

Special Circumstances

Baptism at Mass: If baptism is celebrated within Mass, the deacon is normally not, as noted above, the celebrant of the rite of baptism. But he still has a role to play.[28] The rite of reception should take the place of the greeting and penitential rite and, if it is done at the entrance to the church, the deacon and other ministers would go there with the celebrant and then join in the procession into the church, with the deacon leading the way with the gospel book. He should lead the intercessions, which are taken from the baptismal rite, with petitions added for the church and the world. The baptismal intercessions may be adapted so that they are requests for prayer addressed to the assembly, which is the form that the prayer of the faithful takes at the Eucharist. These will come immediately after the homily, since the Creed is omitted, its place being taken by the entire assembly joining with the parents and godparents in the baptismal promises.[29] The deacon should also provide whatever assistance is needed for the anointing with chrism, the clothing with the white garments, the lighting of the candle, and so forth. At the end of Mass, after the special blessing taken from the baptismal rite, he dismisses the assembly. The two new formulas of dismissal—"Go in peace, glorifying the Lord by your life" and "Go and announce the Gospel of the Lord"—are highly appropriate conclusions for a baptism.

Baptism When One Parent Is Not Christian: Though the church provides a rite for the marriage of a Christian and a non-Christian, it provides no analogous rite for a baptism in which only one of the parents is Christian. Yet this is an increasingly common circumstance. Anyone who has ever celebrated a baptism at which a non-Christian parent is present quickly becomes aware that certain parts of the rite are simply not appropriate as written. While prior to the Second Vatican Council the parents had no role in the baptismal liturgy (indeed, mothers were often not even present), the postconciliar revision of the rite of infant baptism gives a prominent role to the parents of the child. They are now asked if they commit themselves to bringing up their child in the faith; they trace the cross on the child's forehead; they renounce evil and profess their faith; and they may each receive a special blessing at the end that refers to their Christian faith. Some of the prayers presume that they will together be nurturing their child in the faith. When only one parent is Christian, options must be chosen carefully and adaptations must be made, because asking non-Christians to join in these actions is to ask them to pretend to be something they are not.

For example, the deacon alone might mark the child with the sign of the cross, rather than have only one parent join in that ritual. He can use the second form for the final blessing, which prays for the parents but does not mention anything specifically Christian. Only the Christian parent should join with the godparents in the profession of faith, though the non-Christian parent might be asked about his or her willingness to have the child baptized into the faith that has just been professed. Particularly if the non-Christian parent is Jewish, elements of his or her religious tradition might be incorporated—such as the inclusion of readings from the Hebrew Bible or use of the priestly blessing from Numbers 6:24-26—though one should avoid turning the baptism into a syncretistic celebration of natural birth rather than a sacrament of our new birth in Christ.

Of course, such adaptations might prove difficult to do in a celebration in which several families, not all of which include non-Christian parents, are having their children baptized. It might be best to have baptisms in which one parent is not a Christian done separately, though this requires some pastoral delicacy, so that the family does not feel that it is being singled out or excluded.

CHAPTER 5

Making Holy Our Days

In addition to presiding at the baptism of children, deacons also often have a role presiding at other liturgies that form part of the daily and weekly worship of the church. Here I will discuss the three most common occasions when a deacon might preside at such liturgies: the Liturgy of the Hours, the distribution of Holy Communion apart from Mass, and eucharistic exposition and benediction.

The Liturgy of the Hours

At the ordination of a deacon he is asked if he will "celebrate faithfully the Liturgy of the Hours with and for the People of God" (Ordination of Deacons 200). This means that the deacon commits himself not only to praying the Hours privately *for* God's people, but also celebrating them publicly *with* God's people. This might be done on a regular basis—whether before a morning or evening Mass or as a celebration on its own—or on an occasional basis, as part of a parish day of prayer or to begin or conclude a meeting. I will first discuss how a deacon presides at the Hours and then touch on his role in assisting when another presides. I will focus on Morning and Evening Prayer; these directions can be easily adapted for the other offices.

The *General Instruction of the Liturgy of the Hours* (GILH) states, "A priest or deacon should normally preside at every celebration with the people" (254). This might seem a bit of clerical high-handedness, since there is nothing in the Liturgy of the Hours that *requires* the presence of an ordained person,[1] and the word "normally" indicates that a layperson may on occasion preside even if a priest or deacon is present. The preference for an ordained presider underscores that in praying the Liturgy of the Hours one is not simply participating in a form of devotional prayer, but in the official worship of the church. In presiding, the deacon should vest in an alb and stole, particularly if the celebration occurs in a church or chapel (it would seem odd for him to vest for, say, Compline celebrated at the end of a pastoral council meeting in the rectory). The GILH seems to reserve the use of the cope to a priest (255), but since the deacon can wear one when baptizing, it is difficult to understand why he could not wear one for presiding at the Hours, particularly if they were celebrated with great solemnity.

Depending on the setting and the degree of formality, the deacon might either be seated in his chair as the congregation gathers or enter once all have assembled. If the deacon makes a formal entrance, this should be done in silence or perhaps to instrumental music and he should bow to the altar (or genuflect to the tabernacle, if it is in the sanctuary) and venerate the altar with a kiss before going to his seat.[2] He crosses himself as he says, "God, come to my assistance." If using the invitatory at Morning Prayer he makes a small cross over his lips as he says, "Lord, open my lips" (GILH 266). He should make a profound bow at the *Gloria Patri* (i.e., "Glory to the Father . . ."). This opening is fittingly sung. The hymn follows. The hymn given in the Liturgy of the Hours may be used or another hymn may be chosen. It would make sense that the hymn be omitted if it is not sung. Normally all remain standing until the antiphon of the first psalm is said or sung, after which they may sit.

If the psalms and canticles are sung, a cantor should lead their singing if at all possible (GILH 260). If they are recited, the deacon might lead them, though another person could also take this role. The GILH notes with regard to the psalms, "If it is feasible, the sung form is to be preferred" (278). There are many musical settings for the psalms. Some form of chant is both the most traditional and often the most effective way of singing the psalms, though it probably works best with a congregation who prays the Hours often enough to get a feel for the chant.[3] Most hymnals have a number of psalms and canticles set to music and a selection can be made from among these, since it is not required in celebrating the Hours with the people that the psalms appointed for that day be used (GILH 247). Three methods are suggested for both singing and saying the psalms: they may be sung or said by all together; they may be divided between two groups who alternate verses; the antiphon may be used as a response, not unlike the responsorial psalm at Mass (122). Each psalm and canticle ends with the *Gloria Patri* and in some places it is the practice to stand for this and make a profound bow for the first part. The GILH notes that the *Gloria Patri* "is the fitting conclusion that tradition recommends, and it gives to Old Testament prayer a quality of praise linked to a christological and trinitarian interpretation" (123). The prayers at the end of the psalms in the American edition of the Liturgy of the Hours are optional, and in communal recitation might bog the celebration down in too much verbiage. The repetition of the antiphon at the end of the psalms and canticles is optional as well.

The reading should be done by someone other than the presider. Either the short reading found in the Liturgy of the Hours is used, or a longer reading can be selected (GILH 46). A homily can follow the reading, followed by a period of silence (47–48). The deacon who is presiding might give the homily, or it might be given by someone else, including a layperson.[4] Preaching is not essential to the Hours and the homily should probably be briefer than what one would expect at Mass. The responsory after the reading is sung if possible (GILH 281); if it is said, the reader might lead it, since it is a response to the Scripture reading.

All stand for the gospel canticle, which should be sung if at all possible. All make the sign of the cross at the beginning. The altar and the people can be censed during this on particularly solemn occasions. The presider, during the antiphon, puts incense in the thurible. Then, after making the sign of the cross as the canticle begins, he goes to the altar with the thurible and censes it with single swings as at the beginning of Mass, walking around it counterclockwise. Then he may cense the people or he may return to his chair, after which a server censes both him and the people.[5] In some places, instead of censing the altar with a thurible, a brazier of charcoal is placed in front of the altar, with incense put on the coals to burn as the antiphon is sung. This might be appropriate on less solemn occasions or with a smaller congregation.

The intercessions or *preces* can be led by the presider, but are more appropriately led by an assisting minister (GILH 257). The congregation may participate either by making the response provided or by saying the second half of each petition (in which case the response is not said). At the end, a time might be left for the assembly to add its own prayers, either silently or aloud (see 188). The presider then introduces the Lord's Prayer, which is sung or said by all, after which he says the concluding prayer. Then, after greeting the people with "The Lord be with you," he blesses them (on feast days the solemn blessing found in the Missal can be used) and dismisses the people: "Go in peace." Some presiders, in addition to or in place of the dismissal, invite the assembly to exchange the sign of peace. Sometimes at Evening Prayer one of the Marian antiphons from Compline is added, particularly if the group is not going to pray that hour together. If the celebration has been in a church or chapel, the deacon should bow to the altar or genuflect to the tabernacle before departing.

On occasion the Liturgy of the Hours is combined with the celebration of Mass, such that the psalms take the place of the Introductory Rites and the gospel canticle is said or sung following Communion.[6] In such cases it would not be appropriate for the deacon to preside at the part taken from the Liturgy of the Hours and have the priest preside at the Eucharist: the priest should preside over the whole celebration.

Particularly on solemn occasions, the deacon can assist at a celebration of the Hours at which a priest or bishop presides. If the presider wears a cope, the deacon would fittingly be vested in a dalmatic and sit beside the presider. The deacon might do the reading, though this might also be fittingly left for a layperson. The deacon should lead the intercessions and dismiss the people at the end.[7] If any instructions need to be given to the people regarding posture and so forth, this could be done by the deacon as well.

Sunday (and Other) Celebrations in the Absence of a Priest

Due to the shortage in many places of priests to celebrate the Eucharist, deacons are sometimes called upon to preside at liturgies at which Holy Communion is distributed from elements already consecrated.[8] Somewhat confusingly, the church has significantly different provisions for when this occurs on a Sunday and when it occurs on a weekday. I will discuss Sunday celebrations first, and then weekdays.

Sundays

The ritual book *Sunday Celebrations in the Absence of a Priest* (SCAP), developed by the bishops of the United States, is, frankly, a rather odd document, inasmuch as it attempts to provide a normative liturgical framework for what is an anomalous liturgical situation: the separation of Sunday from the celebration of the Eucharist. The bishops write,

> At best these celebrations are only a temporary measure. The community is deprived of the celebration of the Eucharist, and Holy Communion is separated from the Mass. There is a danger of a return to the situation of the past in which the Mass was seen only as a means for providing consecrated hosts for communion.[9]

Consequently, these liturgies, which have as their chief purpose the celebration of the paschal mystery of Christ's dying and rising, are also, by design, marked by a certain sense of absence: the absence of the priest, but even more the absence of the eucharistic sacrifice. Part of the challenge for deacons presiding at these celebrations is to honor the sense of absence they convey, while still helping the assembly to celebrate the presence of the risen Christ.

The deacon should lead the celebration if possible (SCAP 23). It would not be fitting, for example, for a lay pastoral life director to preside and the deacon to assist. The deacon vests in alb, stole, and dalmatic and, as mentioned in chapter 2, does not sit in the presider's chair but in another suitable place, "as a symbol that the community awaits the presence of the priest" (24). Just as at any other liturgy, he should be assisted by readers, servers, cantors, and so forth (25). The church in the United States offers two possibilities for such Sunday celebrations: one a form of the Liturgy of the Hours and the other a Liturgy of the Word; the distribution of Holy Communion may be included in either of these. These forms of celebration are constructed in such a way that they are not simply a Mass with the consecration omitted, in order that there be no confusion between them and the sacrifice of the Mass.

In both forms of celebration, there is to be no entrance procession and the deacon begins with a statement that acknowledges the absence of a priest and the community's consequent inability to celebrate the Eucharist (SCAP 119, 153, 186). When the celebration takes the form of either Morning or Evening Prayer, the Hour then begins as usual with the introduction, hymn, and first psalm. The canticle and second psalm may be omitted. The celebration in the form of a Liturgy of the Word begins with the sign of the cross and a greeting, followed by an opening prayer that is lengthier than the opening prayer used at Mass and incorporates elements of thanksgiving and remembrance reminiscent of the eucharistic prayer. The deacon says this prayer with hands extended and, though no music is provided, it might fittingly be chanted.

In both forms there then follows the Sunday readings appointed for the Eucharist, including the responsorial psalm. The first two readings should be read by readers and the gospel by the deacon. The Book of the Gospels may be used (SCAP 66), and presumably there could be a procession to the ambo with candles and even incense. After the readings, the deacon preaches a homily and the profession of faith is said, either in the form of the Nicene or Apostles' Creed. The prayer of the faithful follows. The rite directs that the deacon, as presider, introduce and conclude the petitions, but an assisting minister reads the intentions (134, 168, 201). If the congregation is used to these intentions being sung at Mass, they could be sung in these celebrations as well. The concluding prayer takes the form of that Sunday's opening prayer from the Roman Missal, which the deacon should pray with hands extended.

If Holy Communion is to be given, in both forms of celebration the deacon then retrieves the Blessed Sacrament from its place of reservation and places it on the altar. There is no mention of singing during this and presumably it is done in silence. The deacon does not remain at the altar but goes to his chair and invites the people to join in singing or saying the Lord's Prayer (SCAP 61). Again, the concern is to distinguish the celebration from the Mass, at which the priest would be standing at the altar. After the Lord's Prayer, which is said without the embolism prayer ("Deliver us Lord . . .") and concluding doxology ("For the kingdom, the power . . .") used at Mass, the deacon goes to the altar, genuflects, and, holding the host slightly raised, invites the people to Communion with the same words used at Mass: "Behold the Lamb of God . . ." Communion is given only under the form of bread (60). The deacon receives Communion first and then proceeds to give Communion to the people, being assisted if need be by extraordinary ministers of Holy Communion (63). There may be singing during the distribution of Communion. Afterward, the deacon or an extraordinary minister returns any of the Blessed Sacrament that remains to the place of reservation.

After Communion, or after the prayer of the faithful if Communion is not given, there is an act of thanksgiving. At Morning and Evening

Prayer this is the gospel canticle with its antiphon (SCAP 58). At a Liturgy of the Word this might take the form of a psalm or hymn (the *Gloria in Excelsis*, which does not form part of the Introductory Rites, is suggested) or a litany. This should ideally be sung by all standing, with the deacon and people facing in the same direction (59). This might be difficult in churches where the seating of the assembly is gathered around three sides of the altar, but presumably the intent is that the deacon be seen as one of the assembly, joining with them in thanking God, and not as someone analogous to the priest standing at the altar for the eucharistic thanksgiving.

Both forms of celebration conclude in the same way. There can be brief announcements and a collection. Then the deacon invites those present to pray for an increase of vocations to the priesthood. Though the rite does not specify this, it would seem to make sense that this invitation be followed by a brief silence. The deacon then blesses the people and may invite them to exchange the sign of peace. The celebration may conclude with a song or instrumental music.

Weekdays

A deacon would most likely find himself distributing Holy Communion outside of Mass on a weekday in the context of ministry in a nursing home or prison or some other place where people have no possibility of attending Mass, since such celebrations are generally discouraged in parishes. The rite for this is found in *Holy Communion and Worship of the Eucharist Outside Mass*, which predates the rite used for Sundays and in some ways does not exhibit the same anxiety over the absence of the priest (indeed, it seems to envision the possibility of a priest using the rite to give Communion to those who could not attend Mass [14, 17]), or the possibility of confusion with the celebration of Mass. At the same time, it also presents a very spare and sober liturgy, largely missing the element of thanksgiving that *Sunday Celebrations in the Absence of a Priest* provides and making no mention of singing except during the distribution of Communion (though it does not forbid it elsewhere either). Presiders are not allowed to incorporate elements from the rite for Sundays into the weekday rite.[10]

The deacon is to vest in alb and stole. There is no procession and the rite begins with a greeting—no mention is made of the opening sign of the cross—and the penitential rite, the texts of which are identical to those found in the Introductory Rites of Mass.[11] There is no provision for the Gloria (which would typically not be used on a weekday in any case) or an opening prayer.

The Liturgy of the Word "takes place as at Mass." This presumably means a first reading, responsorial psalm, possibly a gospel acclamation, and a gospel reading. Another reader should read the first reading and psalm, but the deacon himself should read the gospel, with the usual greeting and announcement. The rite also mentions the possibility of having only one reading, or replacing the psalm with a period of silence.[12] Given how brief the rite is, however, there seems little reason to skimp in this way on the word of God. No specific mention is made of a homily, though if the Liturgy of the Word takes place as at Mass one might presume that a brief homily could be given. The Liturgy of the Word concludes with the prayer of the faithful, which the deacon should introduce and conclude, with an assisting minister announcing the intentions. The opening prayer for the day from the Missal might be used as the concluding prayer of the intercessions.

The deacon then gets the Blessed Sacrament from its place of reservation, places it on the altar, and genuflects. He then prays the Lord's Prayer with the people, apparently still standing at the altar (unlike the rite for Sundays). He may then invite the people to exchange the sign of peace, after which he genuflects, holds up the host, and invites the people to Communion, saying, "Behold the Lamb of God . . ." After receiving Communion himself, he distributes Communion to the people. He then returns the Blessed Sacrament to its place of reservation and after either a period of silence or a song of praise, he says the concluding prayer. He should use one of the prayers from the rite and not use the prayers after Communion found in the Missal, since most of these presume the actual celebration of the Eucharist. He then blesses and dismisses the people as at Mass.

If it is desired to incorporate music into the liturgy, in addition to songs during and after Communion, there might be a song at the beginning, as well as a sung responsorial psalm and gospel acclamation.

Eucharistic Exposition and Benediction

Worship of Christ in the Eucharist apart from Mass developed in the high Middle Ages and was extremely popular up until the Second Vatican Council, after which it suffered something of a decline in popularity. Its popularity was partly a result of it being very much a devotion that was accessible to the people, often incorporating the vernacular and congregational song. Perhaps when, after the council, these things were incorporated into the eucharistic liturgy, there was a correlative loss of interest in these eucharistic devotions. However in recent years there has been a revival of interest in eucharistic adoration, particularly among the young, who have found in it a certain space and silence that balances the relative "busyness" of the reformed rite of Mass. At the same time, the church is careful to stress that "when the faithful honor Christ present in the sacrament, they should remember that this presence is derived from the sacrifice and is directed toward sacramental and spiritual communion."[13]

The distinctive nature of exposition and benediction as rituals that frame an essentially contemplative activity should be kept in mind in presiding at such celebrations. The service itself is extremely flexible and in many ways governed more by custom than by official liturgical books. In what follows, I will describe one common form of exposition, adoration, and benediction. An examination of the liturgical books will indicate those areas where one might depart from what is described.

In preparing for the celebration, the monstrance should be on the altar, usually turned sideways to indicate that it does not yet contain the Blessed Sacrament.[14] A corporal should be on the altar and there should be at least two candles lighted on either side of it, though four or six or even two candelabras are often used. A large host in a lunette should be in the tabernacle.

The deacon should vest in alb or surplice and stole. If the Eucharist is reserved outside the sanctuary, the deacon should wear the humeral veil in bringing it to the altar and be preceded, if possible, by servers with candles.[15] He retrieves the Blessed Sacrament in the lunette from the tabernacle and places it in the monstrance while a Eucharistic hymn is sung. Traditionally, and in my experience almost universally still, this is *O Salutaris Hostia* ("O Saving Victim"). After placing the Blessed Sacrament in the monstrance and turning it to face the people, the deacon kneels before it and censes it with three swings of the censer. The deacon should remain kneeling for at least a brief period of silence after the hymn ends and before any devotions begin.

The period of adoration can be of varying lengths and can take many forms. The Liturgy of the Hours can be prayed. The rosary or some other form of devotional prayer, such as litanies, can be said. Hymns or other songs might be sung. Scripture can be read and a homily or reflection, which can be given by a layperson, might be given. Appreciable periods of silence should be incorporated. Adoration should focus on Christ present in the Eucharist, so a devotion like the Stations of the Cross would not be appropriate. If the Liturgy of the Hours is celebrated, it begins with the introduction, after which the hymn is omitted, since the hymn at the exposition takes its place, and continues through to the intercessions. If incense is used at the gospel canticle, only the Blessed Sacrament is censed. The period of adoration should probably last for at least half an hour, though it might last for several hours and people may come and go (including the deacon), but someone should always be present.

At the end of the period of adoration, Benediction is given and the Blessed Sacrament is reposed. Putting on a white cope, the deacon kneels before the altar and censes the Blessed Sacrament while a hymn is sung—traditionally and almost always *Tantum Ergo* ("Down in Adoration Falling"). He then sings or says one of the prayers given in the rite.[16] Traditionally, this was preceded by the verse and response, "You have given them Bread from heaven / Having all sweetness within it." This is not mentioned in the official rite but in practice is often included. Then, placing the humeral veil around his shoulders, he goes to the altar, takes the monstrance and, facing the people, silently makes the sign of the cross over them. This should be done deliberately, but there is no need for exaggerated slowness. He then replaces the monstrance on the altar and returns the sacrament to the tabernacle. Traditionally, before doing so, he knelt and prayed the Divine Praises ("Blessed be God. Blessed be his Holy Name," etc.). This is still done in some places, though the rite envisions the sacrament being reposed immediately after Benediction. Often the Divine Praises are said as the deacon is reposing the sacrament or afterward (if the deacon is leading them). The celebration concludes with a hymn.

The *Ceremonial of Bishops* states that, when the bishop presides at Exposition and Benediction, the deacon exposes and reposes the sacrament, though the bishop censes the sacrament and gives the Benediction,[17] and presumably a deacon could do this when assisting a priest as well. He might also lead some of the devotions during the period of adoration.

CHAPTER 6

Making Holy Our Years

The liturgical year is one of the great treasures of the Catholic faith. By it Catholics are both formed in the faith by the yearly rehearsal of the mysteries of salvation and enabled to celebrate those mysteries in a way that is extended throughout the year. As the Second Vatican Council's Constitution on the Sacred Liturgy states, "Thus recalling the mysteries of the redemption, [the church] opens up to the faithful the riches of the Lord's powers and merits, so that these are in some way made present at all times; the faithful lay hold of them and are filled with saving grace" (*Sacrosanctum Concilium* 102). The mysteries of Christ's life and work are encompassed in two major "cycles" of celebration: Advent-Christmas, which celebrates the coming of God into our midst, and Lent-Easter, which celebrates the great work of our redemption though the paschal mystery. In addition, the church celebrates the ongoing work of the Spirit through the annual commemoration of the saints on their proper days.

Much of what needs to be said about the liturgical ministry of deacons in these celebrations has already been said in discussing the Eucharist and the Liturgy of the Hours. In this brief chapter I will simply note those celebrations that have distinctive features in which the deacon plays a role. Though the Lent-Easter cycle of feasts is the more ancient and, in some ways, the more significant, I will begin with the Advent-Christmas liturgies because of their relative simplicity, before turning to the somewhat more complex liturgies of the Lent-Easter cycle, and concluding with a few remarks on some unique elements associated with certain saints' days.

Advent-Christmas

One of the struggles of Advent is how to prepare spiritually for the coming of Christ in a season of great secular busyness (and business). One way in which parishes might help people do this is through additional celebrations of the Liturgy of the Hours, particularly Evening Prayer, which can be extremely simple yet prayerful moments when people can pause in the frenetic pace of their days to focus on the Christian mystery of the incarnation. Deacons can have an important role in helping to plan and lead such celebrations. Aside from this, while there are a few distinctive features of Advent in the Eucharist and the Liturgy of the Hours, such as the omission of the Gloria at Mass or the inclusion of the "O" antiphons at Evening Prayer, there is nothing altered or added to the deacon's normal role. Though not strictly speaking a part of the official liturgy, an Advent wreath for use in church can be blessed at Mass, or at Evening Prayer or a celebration of God's word, and in the latter cases a deacon might preside at this blessing.

For the celebration of Christmas itself, in addition to his usual tasks at Mass, the deacon may chant the announcement of the nativity of Christ from the Roman Martyrology, which locates the birth of Christ within the sweep of human history, both sacred and profane (Roman Missal, Appendix I). If the Office of Readings is celebrated immediately before the Mass during the night (sometimes known as "Midnight Mass"), the announcement from the Martyrology is chanted after the responsory of the second reading and is immediately followed by the Gloria in place of the *Te Deum*. If the Office of Readings is not used, the announcement can be chanted before Mass begins, perhaps at the end of the caroling that sometimes precedes Mass. It could be chanted from the ambo or some other appropriate location in the church.[1] The chant is fairly simple, but the deacon should be sure to start low enough that he doesn't need to slip into a falsetto at the end.

The deacon also has an opportunity to exercise his vocal chords on the feast of the Epiphany, with the traditional announcements of the dates of Easter and the other moveable feasts for the coming liturgical year, which the deacon or a cantor may sing between the gospel and the homily. Though it originally had a prosaic purpose of letting people know the dates of important upcoming feasts—something that most of us can find out with a few keystrokes via Google—it also links the Christmas cycle of feasts theologically to the Easter cycle: "Know, dear brothers and sisters, that, as we have rejoiced at the Nativity of our Lord Jesus Christ, so by leave of God's mercy we announce to you also the joy of his Resurrection, who is our Savior" (Appendix I). Not only do the words point us toward Easter, but also the melody echoes the *Exsultet*. Though this proclamation may currently be unfamiliar to many congregations, it can underscore the primacy of Easter in the liturgical year, which can be lost in the secular emphasis on Christmas.

Epiphany is also a traditional time for the blessing of homes, for which the *Book of Blessings* provides a rite (chap. 50, nos. 1597–1621). It may not be practical to bless a large number of homes, but gatherings of families could be organized in a few homes, at which the deacon might preside at the blessing of the host's dwelling. At the end of the blessing, the deacon could follow the ancient tradition of blessing chalk and inscribing the doorway with the year and the initials of the (legendary) names of the three kings (Caspar, Melchior, and Balthasar), thus: 20+C+M+B+16. All of the families present could then take a piece of chalk home with them, so that they can inscribe their own doorways. Unfortunately, the *Book of Blessings* does not provide a prayer for the blessing of chalk, but these are easily found online.[2]

By some reckonings, the Advent-Christmas cycle ends with the feast of the Baptism of the Lord, but in another sense it continues until the feast of the Presentation, which commemorates the bringing of Jesus to the temple forty days after his birth. Because it often falls on a weekday, many Catholics are unfamiliar with the special entrance rite of this feast, which involves the blessing of candles and a procession into the church as the Song of Simeon is sung. The hand candles used by the assembly at the Easter Vigil could be blessed at this time, again linking the Advent-Christmas cycle to the Lent-Easter cycle. The deacon has the role of inviting the congregation to join the procession into the church after the blessing of the candles.

Lent-Easter

Ash Wednesday and Lent

The season of Lent begins with Ash Wednesday, on which all the members of the church join in the penitential act of having ashes imposed on their foreheads. This is done either in the context of the Mass or, in some cases, a celebration of the God's word. When ashes are distributed at Mass, the deacon would fulfill his normal duties, though he should note that there is no penitential rite at the beginning of Mass. The deacon may join in the distribution of the ashes, as may laypeople (*Book of Blessings* 1659). If ashes are distributed outside of Mass, the deacon can, in the absence of a priest, preside at the celebration of God's word. He should vest in alb or surplice and a purple stole and, if desired, a purple cope. The celebration as spelled out in the *Book of Blessings* generally follows the pattern of the Liturgy of the Word at the Mass, omitting the penitential rite at the beginning, and providing a special form of greeting and words of introduction for such celebrations (1661, 1663). After the homily, the deacon blesses the ashes and sprinkles them with holy water (unless they have been blessed at an earlier celebration). The intercessions follow, with the deacon introducing them and an assisting minister announcing the intentions. The deacon concludes the intercessions by inviting all to join in the Lord's Prayer, after which he says a short prayer and blesses the people.

Many of the distinctive liturgical features of Lent itself I have already discussed in chapter 4 in the context of adult initiation. In addition to the rites of the RCIA, the deacon can also help parishioners mark Lent liturgically by presiding at celebrations of the Liturgy of the Hours, eucharistic adoration, and distinctive Lenten devotions such as the Stations of the Cross.

On Palm Sunday the deacon proclaims the palm gospel just as he would the gospel at Mass, and sings or says the words inviting the assembly to join in the procession (if the first form of entry is used). He should walk next to the priest at the end of the procession and fulfill his normal duties during the course of the Mass. Though the deacon can read the passion gospel by himself, traditionally it was proclaimed by three deacons, divided between Christ, the narrator, and the other people; in some cases, the choir took the part of the crowd.[3] If there are three deacons in the parish, they might fulfill this traditional role. If, as is most likely, there are not three deacons, laypeople may take some of the roles, but the deacon should certainly be one of the readers. The deacon should ask the priest's blessing before proclaiming the passion. Note that incense and candles are not used, and the normal greeting and signs of the cross are omitted (Roman Missal, Palm Sunday 21). Everyone kneels for a period of silent prayer after the death of Jesus in the account, and the kneeling and rising of the readers will serve as a signal to the congregation for their own actions, so the readers should be clear about how long they will kneel. At the end of the passion the deacon should say, "The Gospel of the Lord" (with the people responding) and kiss the book as at an ordinary Mass.[4]

The chrism Mass, though traditionally celebrated on the morning of Holy Thursday, is often celebrated on an earlier day of Holy Week. In addition to the consecration of the holy oils, the liturgy focuses on the presbyterate and serves as "a manifestation of the Priests' communion with their Bishop," and the occasion for priests to renew the promises they made at their ordinations (Roman Missal, Chrism Mass 4, 8–9). At the same time, deacons have an important role to play in the liturgy, both by their presence there as ministers within the local church, manifesting its diversity, and in the liturgical action itself. After the renewal of priestly promises, the oils to be blessed or consecrated are brought forward in three vessels carried by deacons, along with the gifts of bread and wine. Laypeople can carry the oil for the sick and for catechumens, but a deacon (or, in the absence of a deacon, a priest) must carry the oil for chrism. Going to the bishop, who is either standing at the altar or at the chair, the first deacon presents his vessel to the bishop and says in a loud voice, "The oil for the holy chrism"; the bishop takes the oil and hands it to another assisting deacon who places it on a table in the center of the sanctuary. The same procedure is followed by the second deacon, saying, "The oil of the sick," and the third, saying "The oil of catechumens."[5] The actual blessing or consecration of the oils may take place at that point, or the oil of the sick may be blessed at the end of the eucharistic prayer and the oil of catechumens and chrism after Communion. If the oil of the sick is blessed at the end of the eucharistic prayer, the deacon who presented it takes the vessel from the table and brings it to the altar, holding it in front of the bishop. At the end of the prayer he returns it to the table. In the procession out at the end, the deacons who carried the vessels may also carry them out, walking immediately behind the processional cross.[6] In many places, however, the oils are not processed out, having already been taken to a place where they can be put into smaller containers for distribution to parishes.

The Triduum
The Mass of the Lord's Supper begins the Sacred Triduum, which the church describes as "the high point of the entire liturgical year."[7]

This Mass has a threefold significance, recalling "the institution of the Eucharist, the institution of the priesthood, and Christ's command of brotherly love."[8] Much of the Mass is like an ordinary festive celebration of the Eucharist, with the addition of the *mandatum* or foot-washing ritual, and the transfer of the Holy Eucharist to a separate place of reservation for adoration and for Communion on Good Friday.

The washing of feet, though today a prominent part of the Mass of the Lord's Supper, was only added to this liturgy in 1956; prior to this, though associated with Holy Thursday (thus the name "Maundy Thursday" in some places), it often took place before or after the liturgy, and was not exclusively a clerical act, but was done by abbots and abbesses, kings and queens. To this day, it remains an optional part of the celebration.[9] The rubrics make no mention of the deacon in this ritual, though he might be included among those whose feet are washed, or assist the priest with the pitcher, towel, and bowl needed to carry out the rite. It may be fitting for the deacon to have his feet washed first and then take the role of assisting the celebrant in washing the feet of others, enacting Jesus' command, "as I have done for you, you should also do" (John 13:15). The act of foot washing was shocking to Jesus' disciples; it continues to make some people uncomfortable today. Some parishes have tried to come up with alternative rituals, ranging from hand washing to shoe shining, that seek to "update" Jesus' act of washing feet. If the people of a parish are that uncomfortable with the ritual, it would be better to omit it than to come up with a substitute. The assembly might use the extra time gained by the omission of the rite to reflect on what other commands and actions of Jesus make them uncomfortable.

The transfer of the Eucharist takes place following the prayer after Communion. Prior to this prayer, as Communion is ending, the deacon should put the remaining hosts in a ciborium and leave it on the altar. After the prayer, the deacon should assist the celebrant with putting incense in the thurible and might accompany him as he goes to kneel before the altar and cense the Blessed Sacrament. The deacon, assisted by servers, takes the thurible from the celebrant and places the humeral veil around his shoulders. Using the humeral veil, the celebrant takes up the ciborium as the procession forms. *The Roman Missal* doesn't mention the place of the deacon in this procession, but the *Ceremonial of Bishops* says that deacons come immediately after the cross and candles that lead the procession and ahead of any concelebrating priests. Both the Missal and Ceremonial indicate that those in the procession (or at least the ministers) who are not carrying something else should carry candles, and presumably this applies to the deacon as well.[10] If the place of repose is outside of the main body of the church, the members of the assembly should join in the procession and the deacon may take a role in directing their movement. Upon reaching the place of repose, the deacon may take the ciborium from the celebrant and place it in the tabernacle; after the priest has censed it, the deacon may close the door.[11] After a period of adoration, the deacon can leave with the celebrant. Alternatively, he might stay to help lead devotions during the period of adoration, perhaps leading Compline to conclude the watch before the Blessed Sacrament, which should end by midnight. The deacon might also help with the stripping of the altar in the church, which is carried out without ceremony, but which should be done prayerfully nonetheless.

The celebration of the Office of Readings or Morning Prayer, or both together, is encouraged during the Triduum. Parishes that have a regularly scheduled morning Mass throughout the week have a ready-made congregation for such celebrations.[12] The deacon can preside at those celebrations. Likewise, he might preside at forms of devotion, such as the Stations of the Cross, which are encouraged on Good Friday.[13] He may *not*, however, preside at the Celebration of the Lord's Passion, even if a priest is not available.[14] Some elements of that liturgy, such as individual veneration of a cross, could be incorporated into such devotions, but there should be no attempt to simulate the passion liturgy.

The liturgy of the Celebration of the Lord's Passion has three primary elements: the Liturgy of the Word, the adoration of the cross, and Holy Communion. The deacon has a prominent role in each of these. He should vest in a red dalmatic if one is available. The Missal says that the priest and deacon "go to the altar in silence," which seems to indicate not a procession through the body of the church, but simply entering from the sacristy. The priest and deacon both prostrate themselves before the altar for a period of time as all pray silently. Kneeling is also an option, though it is a less powerful symbol than prostration and should probably only be done if prostration is impossible. Whichever is chosen, both deacon and presider should do the same thing. After rising, they go directly to the chair and the priest says the opening prayer.

The Liturgy of the Word proceeds as at Mass, with the deacon taking part in the proclamation of the passion gospel as on Palm Sunday. After a brief homily, the assembly may be invited to spend a short period of time in silent prayer.[15] If this does not form the conclusion of the homily, it would seem fitting for the deacon to give this invitation.[16] The prayer of the faithful in this liturgy takes a particularly solemn and ancient form, structured as a series of invitations to pray, each followed by a period of silence and then a prayer. The deacon, standing at the ambo, says or sings the invitations to prayer and then may invite the people to kneel for silent prayer, after which he invites them to stand and the priest sings or says the prayer. Alternatively, the people may stand or kneel throughout the entire series of intercessions. The periods of silence should be appreciable without being overly long, giving the assembly sufficient time to pray for the intention that has been announced.

The adoration of the cross seems to have originated in Jerusalem in the fourth century as the veneration of a relic of the true cross. The rubrics speak of a cross and not a crucifix, though in practice many communities use a crucifix. The showing of the cross prior to veneration may take one of two forms. In the first, the deacon, preceded by two servers with candles, brings the veiled cross from the sacristy to the priest in the sanctuary. The priest unveils first the top of the cross, then each of the arms, each time elevating it and singing, "Behold the wood of the cross . . . ," to which the people respond and then kneel for a moment in silent prayer. The rubrics note that the priest "is assisted in singing by the Deacon or, if need be, by the choir."[17] It is not entirely clear what this means, though it seems to indicate that the deacon or the choir can sing along with the priest. The traditional chant melody for this acclamation, which is given as one alternative in the Missal, is a challenging one, so perhaps the idea is that a priest who is not a strong singer could have the support of stronger singers. The second form of showing the cross mirrors the entrance of the paschal candle at the Easter Vigil, with the deacon,[18] accompanied by servers with candles, bringing the cross unveiled from the back of the church to the sanctuary, pausing three times to elevate the cross and sing, "Behold the wood of the cross . . . ," to which the people respond and then kneel for a moment in silent prayer. There is no mention of the deacon receiving support for his singing, so if the traditional chant seems too daunting he should choose the simpler melody provided. The rubric says that "all kneel," which presumably means that the deacon kneels as well. While this might be difficult if the cross he is carrying is large, it can also serve as a signal to the assembly to kneel.

Whichever form of showing is used, the cross is then placed at the entrance of the sanctuary by the deacon, perhaps in a stand or held by servers, for adoration. Genuflecting and kissing are mentioned as forms of adoration, though some may wish simply to touch the cross. The priest venerates the cross first, followed by the deacon and other clergy who are present. The rubrics mention the possibility of the priest removing his shoes and venerating the cross while barefoot; there is no reason why the deacon could not do this as well (though he probably should not do so unless the presider does, lest a gesture of humility turn into an ostentatious show of personal piety). Even if the assembly is large, multiple crosses should not be used for veneration. Rather, after the presider and some of the clergy and laity present have venerated the cross, the presider should take the cross and, standing before the altar, elevate it and invite the people to adore in silence (ibid., 19). At the end of the period of adoration, the deacon carries the cross "to its place at the altar," where it is placed with candles around it (21). Presumably this means that it is placed close to the altar, not actually on the altar. If not all had an opportunity to adore the cross during the liturgy, at the end the cross might be returned to the entrance of the sanctuary and people invited to approach it for individual adoration after the liturgy.

The liturgy of Holy Communion follows the adoration of the cross. A cloth, corporal, and the Missal are placed on the altar. Presumably a server does this, because the deacon should be going to the place of reservation to retrieve the Blessed Sacrament. Wearing a humeral veil and preceded by two servers with candles, he brings it to the altar "by a shorter route" (ibid., 22). This indicates that this should not retrace the procession at the end of the Holy Thursday Mass but should be as simple and direct as possible. The deacon himself places the Blessed Sacrament on the altar and uncovers the ciborium, after which the priest approaches the altar, genuflects, leads the people in the singing or saying of the Lord's Prayer, and gives the invitation to Communion. After Communion, the deacon returns the Blessed Sacrament to its place of repose, which is preferably outside the main body of the church. After the prayer following Communion the deacon invites the people to bow for the prayer over the people. There is no other dismissal and the presider, deacon, and other ministers genuflect to the cross and leave in silence.

The preparation rites that may be celebrated on Holy Saturday are described in chapter 4, above. This is also the day when, in some cultures, foods that will form part of Easter dinner are brought to be blessed (*Book of Blessings* 1701–28). While falling outside of the official liturgical observance of the Triduum, it can become a way of helping parishioners focus on the religious significance of the coming Easter festivities. The deacon could preside at such a blessing.

The Easter Vigil, which the Missal calls "the greatest and most noble of all solemnities" (2), has four parts: the *lucernarium* or service of light, the Liturgy of the Word, the rites of Christian initiation, and the Liturgy of the Eucharist. This is perhaps the most complicated liturgy of the Christian year, and puts great demands on ministers, not least the deacon who is, as we have seen, the one whose ministry is to make sure that all other ministers can carry out their ministries well. It will be important for the deacon to make sure beforehand that everyone, including and especially the priest celebrant, knows his or her role. The presence of the deacon is important enough that the opening rubrics say, "The Priest is usually assisted by a Deacon" (ibid., 6). This liturgy, more than any other, requires the "situational awareness" of the deacon that I spoke of in chapter 2.

The *lucernarium* begins with the ministers and the assembly gathering at the new fire, followed by the greeting of the people and the blessing of the fire. The deacon would fittingly carry the unlighted Easter candle and hold it for the celebrant as he prepares the candle. After the candle is lighted and the priest sings or says his acclamation, the procession forms with the thurifer in front of the paschal candle and everyone else behind. At the door of the church or, if the fire has been lighted indoors, immediately by the fire, the deacon lifts up the candle and sings, "The light of Christ," and the people make their response. The celebrant lights his hand candle from the Easter candle. The deacon moves to the middle of the church and sings the acclamation again, after which "all light their candles from the flame of the paschal candle" (ibid., 16). In practice this means that the deacon holds the candle low enough that several people can light their hand candles from it and then pass the flame to others.[19] The deacon moves to a place in front of the altar and, raising the candle, sings the acclamation a third time. Prior to the reforms following Vatican II the deacon was directed to sing the acclamation beginning on a higher note each time. This is no longer specified in the rubrics, but remains the practice in some places. After singing the acclamation a third time, the deacon places the candle in its stand by the ambo.

After the priest has placed more incense in the thurible, the deacon, if he is singing the Easter Proclamation, asks for his blessing, making the sign of the cross as he receives it. He then goes to the ambo and incenses the book containing the *Exsultet*, just as he would incense the gospel book at Mass, as well as the Easter candle. If a layperson is singing the *Exsultet*, the blessing, and presumably the censing, is omitted. The rubrics say that the celebrant or a concelebrant may sing the Easter proclamation only "in the absence of a Deacon," and that a lay cantor may do this only "because of necessity" (Easter Vigil 19). It is not entirely clear what constitutes "necessity." Certainly a complete inability or unwillingness to sing on the part of the deacon would make it necessary for someone else to sing the *Exsultet*.[20] The *Exsultet*, however, has since the fourth century been the deacon's chant and he should normally be the one who sings it.

The better the deacon understands the *Exsultet*, the better he will proclaim it. It falls into four sections.[21] The first is an introductory call to praise, bidding the church join with all creation in the praise of God, implicitly connecting the light of the candle with the light of God's glory. This introductory section concludes with a plea by the deacon that he, unworthy as he is, might be able to sing the praises of the Easter candle. The second section begins with the same dialogue found before the preface of the eucharistic prayer, indicating this prayer, like that, is an act of thankful remembrance for God's saving work. The outstanding feature of this section, the repeated phrase, "This is the night," makes the audacious claim that the saving events of the exodus and resurrection are not past but present. The third section moves to praise of the Easter candle itself, which is offered as a holy sacrifice of praise to God. The phrase, "the work of bees and of your servants' hands" echoes the prayers at the preparation of the gifts at Mass. The fourth section gives a brief conclusion to the proclamation, adding an eschatological element in the prayer that Christ might find this candle still burning at his return.

The second part of the Vigil is the Liturgy of the Word. The deacon has no specific role to play during the readings from the Old Testament, which rehearse salvation history, though if people are slow to rise for the prayers that follow each reading and its sung response, he might by a gesture or even a verbal sign encourage them to do so. The deacon proclaims the gospel as he would on any other solemn occasion, except that servers do not carry candles in the procession, since the gospel is read by the light of the Easter candle. This might be an occasion on which the gospel could be chanted, to indicate its primacy among all the other Scripture readings.

The deacon's role in the third part, the liturgy of Christian initiation, is described in chapter 4, above. The fourth part, the Liturgy of the Eucharist, should be like any other festal Sunday Eucharist. If there are any neophytes the deacon should minister the chalice at their First Communion. After Communion, when the Blessed Sacrament is returned to the tabernacle, the deacon should take fire from the paschal candle and relight the sanctuary lamp. After the blessing he dismisses the people, adding the double alleluia to the dismissal.

The Easter Season and Pentecost

The most important thing for a deacon to know about the liturgies of Easter is that it is a season of fifty days, lasting through Pentecost, and that the Sunday liturgies in particular should reflect the joy that flows from the resurrection (or course, all liturgies should do that, but these in particular). At Mass, the rite of blessing and sprinkling with holy water may replace the penitential rite (but not on Easter Sunday, when it follows the renewal of baptismal vows, after the homily). The deacon should remember to include the neophytes in the prayer of the faithful. A parish may also wish to mark the Easter season with special celebrations of the Liturgy of the Hours, at which the deacon might preside. Also, Easter, like Epiphany, is a traditional time for blessing the homes of the faithful, and gatherings for this purpose could be arranged during Easter season.[22] Water blessed at such gatherings could be shared with all who attend, so that they can bless their own homes.

Saints' Days

In addition to the two great annual cycles of Advent-Christmas and Lent-Easter, the church also celebrates the annual feasts of the saints. Most saints' days are distinguished in the liturgy of the church by their proper prayers and readings, which are more the concern of the presider than of the deacon. There are some saints' days, however, that have popular devotions and folk customs that the deacon can assist the assembly in observing. The following are only a few of the most prominent.

The feast of St. Blase (February 3) is a traditional day for blessing throats, which may be done at Mass, after the homily, or as part of a celebration of God's word. The blessing is given by placing two candles that have been joined together in the form of a cross around each person's throat and saying the prescribed formula of blessing (*Book of Blessings* 1633). In some places this blessing is also given on the Sunday following the feast of St. Blase, in which case it is usually given at the end of Mass, after the final hymn. In blessing the person, the deacon should hold the candles to his or her throat with his left hand and make the sign of the cross with his right.

On the solemnity of St. Joseph (March 19), it is the tradition in Italian and Italian-American communities to bless foods, especially pastries, most of which are to be shared with the poor. Sometimes this involves a tableau with people playing the role of the Holy Family and a buffet meal in which all are invited to share (ibid., 1679–1700). Here folk custom and concern for the poor can come together, and it would be appropriate for the deacon, by virtue of his ministry of charity, to encourage such celebrations and to preside at the blessing of food.

There is currently a cultural fascination with various Latino customs surrounding All Souls' Day (November 2), commonly known as *Dia de Muertos* (Day of the Dead). The church can use this fascination to encourage this as a day to visit cemeteries to pray for and honor deceased relatives. The deacon might preside at a service in the cemetery at which Scripture is read, prayers are said, and the litany of the saints is sung as the graves are sprinkled with holy water (ibid., 1734–54).

Among the saints, Mary is preeminent. It is common, in addition to observing the various feasts of Mary in the calendar, to set aside May as a month to honor Mary. Though this can compete somewhat with the Easter season, such things as special Marian hymns at Mass are not inappropriate (particularly Easter-themed ones, like the traditional *Regina Caeli*). It is also traditional to hold a "May Crowning." There is no official rite for this, but a typical celebration, at which the deacon could preside, involves the placing of a statue of Mary on a pedestal, singing a Marian hymn, reading one or more passages of Scripture, offering prayers that invoke Mary's intercession (such as the Litany of Loreto), then crowning the image while a hymn is sung (a traditional choice is "Bring Flowers of the Rarest," but this might prove a bit too sentimental for some), concluding with the Hail Mary.

CHAPTER 7

Making Holy Our Lives

Liturgical worship is woven throughout the lives of Catholic Christians, not only in the rhythms of the day and week and year, but also in the key events of the life cycle. The baptism of infants, though primarily the beginning of the child's initiation as a Christian, also serves to mark his or her arrival in the world. The church is present at other key moments as well: marking milestones to adulthood (as in *Quinceañera* celebrations), celebrating marriages, ordaining clergy and consecrating religious, blessing new homes, observing wedding anniversaries, ministering during illnesses, mourning for the dead. All of these can and should be marked liturgically, and the deacon has a role to play. In this chapter I will focus on four points in the lives of Catholics that have particular significance: marriage, ordination, illness, and death.

Weddings

Weddings have a bit of a bad reputation among clergy. From "bridezillas" (in my experience, more legendary than real) to intoxicated best men to tiny ring bearers and flower girls who do fine at the rehearsal and fall apart at the ceremony, there are numerous reasons why one will hear priests and deacons say that they would rather do a hundred funerals than a single wedding. Depending on one's pastoral situation, one might feel only loosely connected to the couple, who themselves are often fairly loosely connected to the church. I can think of all too many instances when I've asked, in the course of conducting the official prenuptial investigation, "Are you currently a practicing Catholic?" and seen a look of panic in the potential bride or groom's eyes. "Um, well . . . I . . . um . . . kind of . . ." Many people who come to the church for marriage have not been particularly fervent practitioners of their faith, at least in recent years, yet something has drawn them: a desire to please their parents, a sense of tradition, a perhaps vague feeling that they want God involved in their married life, a nascent resolution to practice their faith together as a family. It is precisely for this reason that weddings provide a wonderful pastoral opportunity to present the Christian faith to people at a key turning point in their life, and one element of this is to celebrate well the liturgy of marriage.

Indeed, the actual planning of the ceremony can become an important occasion to engage the couple on questions of faith: Which Scripture reading would they like to use? Why did those particular readings speak to them? Do they want to present flowers at Mary's altar? What significance does Mary have for them? What cultural customs surrounding weddings (e.g., fathers "giving away" brides, lighting a "unity candle") do they see as significant and how do those customs fit with the church's understanding of marriage? It is important for the deacon to bear in mind, and to remind the couple, that much of what people associate with weddings is highly culturally specific and is ruled by custom (or bridal magazines) and not by the rite of marriage itself. Though most parishes have written guidelines that couples are given at the outset, it never hurts while planning to remind them that secular readings and pop songs are not allowed as part of the ceremony. These sorts of discussions can impress on the couple the church's view of marriage and the seriousness with which they should engage it. Make sure the ceremony is planned far enough ahead of time that expectations concerning readings, music, decorations, and so forth can be adjusted if need be.

In the Western Catholic theology of marriage, it is the couple who, by their vows, are the ministers of the sacrament of matrimony. In presiding over a wedding ceremony, the deacon should bear in mind that his role is to witness the wedding and to receive the bride and groom's consent on behalf of the church. Under special circumstances, some dioceses will allow a deacon to preside at the exchange of consent at a nuptial Mass (reserving the nuptial blessing for the priest celebrant), but the majority of weddings at which a deacon presides will be celebrated outside of Mass. There are two forms provided for this, one for when both bride and groom are baptized (whether in the Catholic Church or another Christian tradition), and one for when one of them is not baptized. Deacons should be careful to use the proper rite, since there are some subtle but important differences in the wording.[1]

At the rehearsal, the deacon should have as his chief aim to make sure that all the participants feel comfortable enough in their roles to be able to enter into the wedding liturgy without anxiety. He should physically walk the wedding party through the ceremony, so they will have a clear idea of where to stand, sit, and so forth. He should also make sure that readers practice their readings, so that they can be aware of any acoustical peculiarities that the particular space may possess. Many readers at weddings are not trained lectors and will need to be reminded to read more slowly than might initially feel natural to them.

For the wedding, the deacon vests in alb or surplice and stole. He may also wear a dalmatic. If he is going to sprinkle the rings when blessing them, he should have holy water ready and may wish to have a small plate on which the rings can be placed at the appropriate time. He should also check to make sure that any special seating needed for the bride and groom and the wedding party is in place. The last minutes before the wedding begins can often be taken up with questions from photographers, wedding planners, and even guests looking for the restrooms; the deacon should behave charitably and helpfully in all such interactions without losing his focus on the liturgy that is about to take place.

Entrance and Liturgy of the Word

The Order of Celebrating Matrimony (OCM) prescribes that the deacon will either go to the door of the church to welcome the bride and groom and then enter with them in procession (something rarely seen in the United States), or enter from the sacristy and stand at his place as the couple enters in procession, welcoming them after the procession arrives at the sanctuary (80–81, 83–84). In some places, the deacon, the groom, and the groomsmen enter together from the sacristy and only the bride processes, escorted by her father and another male relative. There is no formal "giving away" of the bride in a Catholic wedding, though it might be appropriate for the groom to meet the bride at the entrance to the sanctuary, shake hands with her father, give her time to kiss him, and then the two of them enter the sanctuary together and stand before the deacon, with the bride, by tradition, on the deacon's right and the groom on his left.

It is often a challenge to get congregations at weddings to sing, but even if there is to be singing it is probably better to have this procession accompanied by instrumental music, since everyone will be more interested in looking at the bride than in singing. If an opening hymn is desired, it can be sung once the bride reaches the sanctuary.

Once the bride and groom have arrived at the sanctuary, the deacon bows to the altar and venerates it with a kiss (OCM 82, 85). The second edition of the OCM directs that he then go to the chair, but depending on the arrangement of the sanctuary we may wish to remain standing in front of the bride and groom. The deacon makes the sign of the cross and greets the assembly with one of the greetings used at Mass. The deacon should keep his expectations low as to the participation of the assembly in responding to this and other greetings. For whatever reason, people who know the proper responses at Mass seem to forget them at weddings. He offers a general welcome using one of the forms provided in the OCM (87–88) "or similar words," and then says the opening prayer. He should then invite everyone to sit and may need to invite the first reader to come forward.

The OCM says that the Liturgy of the Word follows "in the usual manner" (90). This presumably means that it will take the form that it does at Mass, with one or two readings in addition to the gospel, along with a responsorial psalm and (if sung) a gospel acclamation. The second edition of the OCM specifies that at least one reading must make a direct reference to marriage. The deacon may well have to ask the people to stand for the gospel reading and should be prepared to make the responses to the announcement of the gospel himself. For the homily, the deacon can incorporate some of what the couple shared with him during the planning of the ceremony about the significance of the readings to them. After the homily the deacon should allow for a brief period of silence.

The Rite of Marriage

The deacon invites the bride and groom to return to their places in the sanctuary and to stand facing him. They should not yet join hands (though this might be their natural inclination) during the deacon's address to them and the three questions he asks them concerning their intentions in entering into marriage. To each of the questions they should answer individually for themselves. He then invites them to join hands for the exchange of vows. In joining hands, they should naturally turn and face each other.

There are two different forms of the vows in the United States and the deacon should determine ahead of time which of them the couple wishes to use. On occasion a couple may ask to write their own vows. This is not an option offered by the rite. If, however, a couple feels strongly that they want to speak their own words of promise to each other, this should be done in addition to the official vows, before their exchange.

He should also determine ahead of time how they wish to exchange the vows. There are different possibilities:

> reciting them from memory
> reading them
> repeating them, clause by clause, after the deacon
> answering "I do" to the vows posed as a question by the deacon

The first two options underscore the role of the couple as the ministers of the sacrament of marriage by allowing the deacon to fade into the background. If the couple chooses to memorize the vows, the deacon should be ready to prompt them if they forget. If they read the vows, the deacon should print them out in a large font so that they can see them easily. The option of responding "I do" to the vows posed as questions might be appropriate in some circumstances, such as when one of the couple is not comfortable speaking in English. The deacon then speaks the words by which he receives their consent, for which the second edition of the OCM provides two forms. He might place his hand over the couple's joined hands as a visual sign of sealing their consent. An acclamation of praise by the congregation follows, which the deacon must figure out how to prompt.

Typically the best man has the wedding rings. The rings can be placed on a small plate, which the best man or a server holds while the deacon blesses them, perhaps sprinkling them with holy water. The words at the exchange of the rings can be memorized by the couple or read by them or they can repeat them after the deacon. In the marriage of a Christian and a non-Christian the reference to the Trinity can be omitted (OCM 132). Sometimes after the exchange of rings an additional ritual is inserted. The OCM makes provision for the Mexican custom of exchanging the *arras* or gold coins (101B). Other rituals, such as the unity candle or the mixing of colored sand, are not found in the OCM and the deacon should feel free to suggest that they might be incorporated into the reception rather than the ceremony. The presentation of flowers at the altar of the Virgin Mary, a long-standing tradition though not an official part of the rite, could occur at this point or after the final blessing. In either case, the deacon should encourage both the bride and groom to take part in this presentation, though of course no one should feel compelled to participate in a ritual that one does not believe in. Prie-dieux can be placed in front of the altar of Mary for the couple to kneel on and pray. The deacon can suggest during the ceremony planning that the Hail Mary might be an appropriate prayer for them to say as they kneel there.

The prayer of the faithful follows. The deacon should invite the congregation to stand. The couple may wish to write the intentions themselves or the deacon can prepare them, discussing with the couple during the planning of the ceremony any special intentions that they want included. After the deacon gives the invitation to prayer, at the end of which he should announce what the response will be, the intentions can be read by a layperson or, if need be, by the deacon himself. After the deacon says the concluding prayer, the Lord's Prayer follows. The second edition of the OCM provides a special invitation for the wedding of a Christian and a non-Christian that seeks to respect the consciences of the non-Christians present: "God the Father wills that his children be of one heart in charity; / let those who are Christian call upon him / in the prayer of God's family, / which our Lord Jesus Christ has taught us" (OCM 136).

The bride and groom ordinarily kneel for the nuptial blessing, though in the marriage of a Christian and a non-Christian they may stand (138). The second edition of the OCM makes optional provision for the Latin custom placing of the *lazo* (i.e., a wedding garland) or a veil over the shoulders of the couple prior to the nuptial blessing. There are three forms of the nuptial blessing provided for weddings in which both the bride and groom are baptized and one for when one of them is unbaptized. In the latter case, the OCM allows for the omission of the nuptial blessing entirely, with a brief prayer over the bride and groom being substituted (140). The second edition of the OCM provides music for this blessing. The chanting of the nuptial blessing would provide a suitably solemn climax to the marriage rite.

The ceremony concludes with a final blessing for the congregation, after which many deacons introduce the new couple. If he does this, he should discuss with them how they would like to be introduced. Not every couple wants to be introduced as Mr. and Mrs. [husband's name]. Typically, the congregation will at this point show their approval by applause, during which the couple can kiss. There is no need for the deacon to say, "You may now kiss the bride," as if the groom had been waiting for this moment to gain that privilege.

Ordinations

Because ordinations are diocese-wide events, a deacon doesn't really have to know a lot about them: if you are serving a liturgical role, someone will let you know in detail what you are supposed to do, and will probably be present during the liturgy itself to lead you around. Taking place in the context of Mass, much of what the deacon needs to do at an ordination has been covered in chapter 3.

An ordination will typically have at least three deacons serving at it: one to read the gospel and two to attend the bishop and fulfill other diaconal roles. At diaconal ordinations at least some of the newly ordained will fulfill their diaconal role in the Liturgy of the Eucharist. At the ordination of presbyters and deacons, a deacon calls the candidates forward after the gospel[2] and gives the assembly directions to kneel and stand before and after the litany (if it is not a Sunday or during the season of Easter).[3] A deacon may be asked to help vest a newly ordained deacon in stole and dalmatic (ibid., 511). At the ordination of a presbyter or bishop, a deacon may hold the vessel of chrism when the bishop anoints the newly ordained priest's hands or the head of the new bishop. Also at the ordination of a bishop, two deacons, by virtue of their office as heralds of the gospel, hold the open gospel book above the head of the one being ordained during the prayer of consecration (583).

At the ordination of a deacon, typically all of the deacons of a diocese will attend in vestments and will exchange the kiss of peace with the newly ordained deacons at the end of the ordination rite, after the handing over of the Book of the Gospels and before the presentation of the gifts (513). Though the sign of peace serves here as a joyous welcome of the newly ordained into the diaconate, it is not the occasion for what the master of ceremonies at my own ordination called "promiscuous backslapping" (something to which men are prone, which somehow makes them feel better about embracing each other). At a presbyteral ordination, deacons who are not serving the liturgy may or may not be invited to vest and sit with the clergy; practice differs from diocese to diocese.

Ministry to the Sick and Dying

Though deacons cannot administer the sacrament of the anointing of the sick,[4] they have an important role to play in the pastoral care of the sick and the dying. Deacons often serve as hospital chaplains or visit the hospitalized and homebound, and so should be familiar with the provisions of the ritual book *Pastoral Care of the Sick*. Ministry to the sick is one of the places where the deacon's ministry of liturgy and his ministry of charity come together most intimately.

Perhaps the most common liturgical ministry to the sick carried out by deacons is bringing them the Eucharist. *Pastoral Care of the Sick* notes that in bringing Communion to those who would otherwise be deprived of it, "the minister of communion represents Christ and manifests faith and charity on behalf of the whole community toward those who cannot be present at the eucharist" (73). If possible, a table should be prepared with a lighted candle. Upon arriving in the home or hospital room, the deacon greets those present and may sprinkle them with holy water. There follows a penitential rite: either the *Kyrie* with invocations or the *Confiteor*. Then there is a reading from Scripture, done by the deacon or someone else. Within the rite three gospel passages are offered, which presumably would be read by the deacon, using the usual greeting and announcement, but the option of other readings is offered as well (ibid., 84). Particularly on a Sunday or holy day it might be appropriate to use the gospel appointed for that day. The deacon may offer a few remarks on the reading, oriented toward the needs of the sick person and his or her caregivers. Intercessions may be offered, with someone other than the deacon announcing the intentions. The litany from the liturgy of anointing would be appropriate (121), or the deacon might prepare intentions beforehand.

The Lord's Prayer follows and then the invitation to Communion, for which two forms are given: the usual one from the Mass, "Behold the Lamb of God . . . ," and "This is the bread of life. Taste and see that the Lord is good." To both of these the usual response from the

Mass is made. After this Communion is given. The sick person may need to receive Communion under the form of wine alone, in which case provision will need to be made beforehand for the Blood of Christ to be reserved in a sealed container. The deacon should consume any that remains (ibid., 74). After a period of silence the deacon says the concluding prayer and the blessing.

This describes the full celebration of Communion for the sick. Obviously, the condition of the sick person will need to be taken into account and some elements abridged depending on the person's stamina (ibid., 40). In the case of giving Communion to a large number of patients in their rooms in a hospital or other institution, the minimal rite is simply the invitation to Communion and the reception of Holy Communion, with a concluding prayer said in the last room visited. It is difficult to imagine a nonemergency situation that would call for such severe minimalism, and ministers are encouraged in particular to have a brief reading from Scripture and the Lord's Prayer prior to Communion (93–94). Some prayer after Communion, whether one provided by the rite or an extempore one by the deacon addressed to the patient's particular needs, would also seem appropriate.

Though deacons can neither anoint nor hear confessions, and so cannot perform the full "last rites," they can give Communion for the dying or Viaticum, which some scholars argue is the oldest and most important component of the rites for the dying (ibid., 20).[5] A special rite is provided for this, which includes near the beginning an address to those present that speaks of the Eucharist as "this food for our journey" (199). A selection of brief gospel passages is provided. If possible, the dying person renews his baptismal promises, followed by an optional brief litany and the Lord's Prayer. The minister then gives the invitation to Communion, for which a special form is provided: "Jesus Christ is the food for our journey; / he calls us to the heavenly table." Immediately after the sick person receives Communion, the deacon says, "May the Lord Jesus Christ protect you / and lead you to eternal life" (207a, 193). Should the dying person linger, he or she can receive the Eucharist as Viaticum on repeated occasions, "frequently if not daily" (183). Because time is often short when someone is in extremis, the deacon should familiarize himself in advance with this rite, as well as the prayers for the dying that are contained in *Pastoral Care of the Sick*.

Deacons can also play a role in communal celebrations of anointing: leading the third form of the penitential rite, reading the gospel, leading the litany before the anointing, and, if the celebration occurs within the context of the Eucharist, fulfilling his normal duties at Mass. In situations where a deacon has been regularly visiting someone who is homebound or in the hospital, or where he serves as a chaplain in a hospital or other institution, it would be fitting for him to accompany a priest who comes to provide the sacrament of anointing so that a reassuringly familiar face might be present. On these occasions, even when the abbreviated form is used for patients in their rooms, the deacon might read a brief passage from Scripture and offer the litany for anointing.

Rites for the Dead

The *Order of Christian Funerals* states, "The Church calls each member of Christ's Body—priest, deacon, layperson—to participate in the ministry of consolation: to care for the dying, to pray for the dead, to comfort those who mourn" (8). Liturgically speaking, the most common ways in which deacons share in the ministry of consolation is through conducting wake services and serving at funeral Masses and committals. Less commonly (though in some places with increasing frequency) a deacon might preside at a funeral liturgy celebrated outside of Mass or at the committal in the cemetery. I will look briefly at each of these.

Similar issues can arise in the planning of the rites for the dead as in the planning of wedding ceremonies, though within a much shorter time frame and with heightened emotions. Families may have a favorite biblical passage or poem or song that they wish to be incorporated. A deacon who is assisting the family will have to exercise a degree of pastoral judgment regarding whether and how to honor such requests. Some music may simply be unsuitable for Christian liturgy (e.g., Journey's "Don't Stop Believin'" or the Notre Dame fight song), while other musical requests might not represent the deacon's own taste but still express appropriate themes for the burial of a Christian. A poem should never replace a reading from Scripture, but might be read during the remembrances at a vigil service. A general rule of thumb is that the grieving family should be accommodated as much as possible without compromising the integrity of the funeral rites.

Another pastoral issue is the question of cremation. The preference of the church is for the body to be buried intact. Even if the family should choose to have the body cremated, they can be encouraged to have this take place after the funeral liturgy, so that the body may be present at the vigil and the liturgy, which "allows for the appropriate reverences for the sacredness of the body at the Funeral Mass."[6] Should cremation take place before the funeral, the presider should use the adapted texts provided in an appendix to the *Order of Christian Funerals* (OCF). The US bishops note, "The practice of scattering cremated remains on the sea, from the air, or on the ground, or keeping cremated remains in the home of a relative or friend of the deceased are not the reverent disposition that the Church requires" (OCF Appendix 2, 417). Communicating these things to grieving families can require considerable pastoral delicacy.

Wakes

What is commonly called a "wake service" is more properly known as a "vigil." The provisions of the *Order of Christian Funerals* are somewhat at odds with American custom, for which the wake is more a time of friends and family visiting with survivors at the funeral home in order to "pay their respects" than it is an occasion for liturgical prayer. Some families, though increasingly few, expect that what prayer there is will take the form chiefly of the rosary or some other sort of devotional prayer. The church, however, expects either a vigil service with a Liturgy of the Word, or some portion of the Liturgy of the Hours. If the deacon has the role of working with the family to plan the wake, he might gently suggest to the family some of the advantages of the rites provided by the church, not least of which is greater accessibility to non-Catholics and those Catholics for whom the rosary is not a familiar devotion. There is, of course, nothing to prevent the rosary or other prayer from occurring earlier during the time of visitation.

Vigil services typically take place at funeral homes, though they might also take place in the home or at church. The deacon is directed to vest "according to local custom." Different dioceses offer different guidance: some suggest alb and stole, others simply coat and tie; in some dioceses the funeral vigil is one of the occasions specified when the deacon might wear a clerical collar. The rite specifies that if the vigil takes place at church, the deacon should vest in alb or surplice and stole (OCF 66). If the stole is worn, it may be white, purple, or black (39). White is by far the most common color in the United States, and is mandated in some dioceses, though purple is quite common for funerals in Europe. It is also possible to use purple for the vigil and white for the funeral Mass and committal.

When vigils are celebrated in funeral homes, they typically come at the end of the period of visitation. If the coffin is open for viewing, it may remain open. If the vigil is celebrated in a church where the funeral Mass will be, the rites for the reception of the body, described below in the context of the funeral service, take place at this time (OCF 55, 58).

The vigil begins with a greeting and opening song. The rite stresses the importance of singing this song (OCF 68), so something extremely familiar and easily sung without accompaniment is best. The deacon then invites those present to pray and, after a period of silence, says the opening prayer. The rite suggests two readings: the first reading done by a layperson and the gospel reading done by the deacon, with a responsorial psalm in between (59). If possible, the responsorial psalm should be sung. The deacon should give a brief homily, "to help those present find strength and hope in God's saving word" (61). In other words, the homily is not the time for remembrance of the deceased, but to open up God's word to comfort those who mourn. After the homily, there is a litany of intercession, which the deacon should introduce, but which could be read by someone else, if this seems appropriate. The Our Father and a concluding prayer follow.

At this point the rite provides for words of remembrance. Some dioceses forbid, or at least strongly discourage, eulogies at funerals, so the vigil can become the occasion for family and friends to offer their memories of the deceased. People might be asked ahead of time to offer a few words, but the occasion can also be opened up to any who might feel moved to speak (an advantage of having such remembrances at the vigil rather than the funeral Mass). The rite concludes with a final prayer for the deceased, a final blessing for those present, and, if desired, a song.

If a priest or another deacon presides at the vigil, a deacon should assist by reading the gospel and leading the litany. Instead of or in addition to the vigil liturgy, particularly if there is an extended time of visitation, some part of the Liturgy of the Hours might be celebrated. This would be particularly appropriate if those present at the vigil were familiar with this form of prayer.

Funeral Liturgies Outside of Mass

Though the church prefers that the funeral be celebrated in the context of the Eucharist, there are occasions, typically when there is no priest available, when a deacon will be called upon to preside at a funeral liturgy outside of Mass. On such occasions, efforts should be made to provide for a memorial Mass for the family at some later date.

The liturgy may take place in a church or at a funeral home or a cemetery chapel. The deacon should vest in an alb or surplice and stole. He may also wear a cope (OCF 182). Unless the rite of receiving the body into the church has already been celebrated as a part of the vigil, the deacon and any assisting ministers go to the door of the church, where he meets the body, usually accompanied by members of the family. After the liturgical greeting he may wish to greet the family more personally, particularly if he has not been with them earlier in the day. He sprinkles the coffin with holy water. If the font is near the entry of the church, it would be appropriate to use water taken from the font. Then the pall is placed upon the coffin. Often this is done by members of the family or by friends. The pall is the great equalizer: it makes the bargain basement coffin indistinguishable from the deluxe model. Under no circumstances should a flag of any sort be substituted for the pall. If the family wishes the coffin to be draped with a flag, it can be put on after the coffin leaves the church and the pall is removed (38, 132). Once the pall is in place, the coffin is brought into the church in procession, with the deacon and any assisting ministers preceding the coffin and mourners, and placed before the altar, where the Easter candle is burning. A hymn or other song is sung during the procession. Christian symbols such as a Bible or a cross may be carried in procession as well and placed on the coffin once it is in place. If there is no reception of the body, the liturgy begins with the opening song.

After an expanded invitation to prayer, the deacon prays the opening prayer and the Liturgy of the Word proceeds as it would at Mass, with the deacon reading the gospel. The deacon should give the homily, which is always a reflection on Christian hope in light of the Scriptures and, as the *Order of Christian Funerals* notes, "never any kind of eulogy" (141). The prayer of the faithful follows, which the deacon should introduce and conclude, with the intentions read by an assisting minister or one of the family or friends present at the funeral. The deacon then leads all in praying the Lord's Prayer.

The rite makes provision for Communion for the reserved sacrament, though this is strongly discouraged in some dioceses. If Communion is given, the deacon should get the Blessed Sacrament from its place of reservation prior to the Lord's Prayer and place it on the altar. After the Lord's Prayer, he gives the invitation to Communion as at Mass and, after receiving Communion himself, distributes Communion to the people. He then returns the Blessed Sacrament to the tabernacle and says the prayer after Communion.

If the final commendation is to take place as part of the rite of committal, the deacon invites the assembly to depart for the place of burial and all leave in procession. If some of those present at the funeral will not be going to the place of committal, then it is better to have the commendation form the conclusion of the funeral liturgy. The deacon invites all to pray, after which there is a period of silence. A song of farewell is then sung, during which the deacon incenses the body, walking around the coffin. He then says the prayer of commendation and invites all to depart for the place of burial. As the procession leaves the church, the chant *In Paradisum* is traditionally sung, though another song can be substituted.

Rite of Committal

The rite of committal is the "graveside service" that forms the conclusion of the funeral rites. It is, the *Order of Christian Funerals* notes, "a stark and powerful expression" of "the separation in this life of the mourners from the deceased" (213). It is a ritual that stares the loss caused by death in the face and dares to offer Christian hope. Even when a funeral Mass is celebrated, a deacon may be asked to preside over this part of the funeral rites. He could vest in alb or surplice and stole, or may wear other suitable clothing. The rite often takes place at the graveside, or in a chapel at the cemetery, particularly if the actual interment is not to take place immediately.

The deacon begins with an invitation to all those present to pray for the deceased and for themselves. There then follows a short Scripture reading and a prayer over the place of committal. If the commendation did not form part of the funeral liturgy, it follows at this point. The deacon then says the words of committal. The coffin might be lowered into the ground at this point, or after the rite has concluded. The deacon introduces the intercessions, with the intentions read by an assisting minister, or one of the family or friends present at the funeral, or if need be by the deacon himself. The rite ends with a con-cluding prayer, a prayer over the people, a final prayer for the deceased, a blessing, and a dismissal. A final song—something very familiar that could be sung without hymnals—might conclude the celebration. During or after the song, gestures of leave-taking may take place, such as those present each sprinkling the casket with holy water or placing a small amount of earth in the grave (if the coffin has already been placed there).

Assisting at the Funeral Mass and Rite of Committal

Celebrating the funeral liturgy in the context of the Eucharist is the preferred option of the church, for in the Eucharist the Christian com-munity "offers the Father in the Spirit the eucharistic sacrifice of Christ's Passover from death to life" and in Holy Communion experi-ences "a foretaste of the heavenly banquet that awaits them" (OCF 154). During the funeral Mass, the deacon should perform his ordinary duties. In addition, he might assist the family with the placing of the pall and announce the procession to the place of committal after the commendation (if this is to occur immediately following the funeral). He may also be asked to give the homily. During the committal, he should lead the litany of intercession, invite those present to bow their heads for the concluding prayer over the people, and dismiss them at the end.

CHAPTER 8

Liturgy and the Spiritual Life of the Deacon

Much of this book has been taken up with practical advice intended to help the deacon assist and preside at the various liturgies of the church. I have attempted not only to explain *what* the deacon should do but also to explain *why* things are done in the way that they are done. Leadership and ministry in the liturgy is not only a matter of doing things right, but of doing them intelligently, doing them because we have some idea of the reason for doing them that way. Liturgical ministry intelligently engaged in helps to foster among all the faithful what the Second Vatican Council called "that full, conscious, and active part in liturgical celebrations which is demanded by the very nature of the liturgy" (*Sacrosanctum Concilium* 14). Such intelligent liturgical participation will also affect the spirituality of the deacon. Indeed, by virtue of his ordination and his call to the ministry of liturgy, the deacon is called to develop a distinctively "liturgical" spirituality, that is, a spirituality grounded in and nourished by participation in the rites and liturgies of the church. While there is much that could be said about what a liturgical spirituality is, here I will discuss briefly only three aspects: the spiritual challenges posed by ministering in the liturgy, the spirituality of the Liturgy of the Hours, and the way in which the words and actions of the liturgy shape and form our spiritual lives.

The Spirituality of Liturgical Ministry

I have heard a number of deacons say that once they began taking a public ministerial role at Mass, they could not pray at Mass in the way they did before; I have even heard some say that they no longer find Mass a prayerful experience. If this is in fact the case, then we have a serious problem, since this would mean the deacons and other ministers are simply actors fulfilling a role, rather than members of the praying assembly. There are a few things that might be said in response that will point the way to a spirituality of liturgical ministry.

First, one issue is what we mean by "prayer." For deacons especially, those points in the liturgy that many people use for quiet, prayerful reflection—before Mass begins, during the preparation of the gifts, during and after Communion—are times when they tend to be quite busy. Inasmuch as we associate "prayerfulness" with closing our eyes and shutting out surrounding sights and sounds, there is very little time for a deacon to be prayerful in the liturgy. But of course we might need to question what we mean by "prayerful." Is reading the gospel in a way that makes it come to life for our listeners because it has come to life within us not prayerful? Is listening attentively as the celebrant proclaims the eucharistic prayer in our name not prayerful? Is the care we show during Holy Communion to the Body and Blood of Christ, present both in the Eucharist and in those receiving the Eucharist, not prayerful? In all of these things we are showing honor to God, which is the ultimate purpose of prayer.

Second, even if we mean by "prayerful" something restricted to quiet reflection, the liturgy should be structured in such a way that the assembly and its ministers can be united together in moments of silence: after the readings or the homily or Communion. Of course, the deacon should never completely abandon his situational aware-ness, since something might arise during a period of silence that he needs to attend to. But the liturgy should have a rhythm to it that provides for moments of slackening in the liturgical action, when the entire assembly, people and ministers together, have nothing on the liturgical agenda except to let the Spirit move.

Third, though liturgies should incorporate periods of silence, they do not exist primarily as occasions for private prayer, and particularly not for the ministers. If we understand this, there are two conclusions we might draw from it. On the one hand, deacons need to realize that they are ordained to serve the assembly, and whatever loss of quiet prayer during the liturgy that they experience should be treated as a spiritual sacrifice offered to God. Candidates for the diaconate who find themselves spiritually desolate during their formation because their liturgical ministry interferes with their praying should probably reexamine their call to the diaconate. On the other hand, a deacon who finds his liturgical ministry interfering with his prayer life might ask whether he is spending enough time in prayer outside the liturgy, or is overburdening the liturgy with his spiritual expectations.

Finally, deacons might consider occasionally attending liturgies and not serving. It is true that *The General Instruction of the Roman Missal* states, "When he is present at the celebration of the Eucharist, a Deacon should exercise his ministry, wearing sacred vestments" (171).[1] This directive reflects the truth that one always participates liturgically according to one's place within the *ordo* of the church, which is not simply functional but is a matter of sacramental identity. But it is also true that there may be a psychological and spiritual need for the deacon to occasionally be "the person in the pews," whether at the Eucharist or at a celebration of the Hours. This might particularly be the case for deacons who are married and would benefit from sitting with their families on occasion. Or for those many deacons who have secular employment and may try to fit daily Mass into a lunch hour or right before or after work, the extra minutes needed to vest and prepare to minister might just not be available. There is also, one could argue, something theologically fitting about deacons occasionally worshiping as part of the assembly rather than ministering. Our fundamental sacramental identity is not as ordained clerics (as important as that might be) but as members of the faithful, God's holy baptized people. Particularly when another deacon is already serving, joining the ranks of the faithful on occasion might remind the deacon of his solidarity with them and so help him to better serve them on other occasions.

Praying the Liturgy of the Hours

At their ordination, deacons commit to praying the Liturgy of the Hours or some portion thereof (for permanent deacons, this is typically Morning and Evening Prayer). In chapter 5, I discussed the role of deacons in public celebrations of the Hours, and it is worth underscoring again the important role that deacons can have in fostering such celebrations. Indeed, they will find that communal celebration of the Hours, even in only a small group, can deepen their appreciation of the Hours as a vehicle of prayer, since they are by their very nature a communal form of prayer.

For most deacons, however, most of their praying of the Hours will be in private. Yet it is important to remember that even when praying the Hours alone the deacon's prayer is a public prayer. This is the case because the Liturgy of the Hours is the official prayer of the church, something that one prays in explicit union with the church and with all those who participate in this form of prayer. This is even more the case with a deacon, because he prays the Hours as part of his mandate from the church; it is not a form of prayer that he chooses for himself, but one that is imposed upon him. This might sound somewhat negative, except that it is an imposition that the deacon should joyfully surrender to, in the same way that one would joyfully surrender to the obligations of marriage out of love for one's spouse. One takes on the burden of the Hours out of love for the church, "in order that, at least in their persons, the duty of the whole community [to pray] may be carried out regularly and reliably, and the prayer of Christ continue unceasingly in the Church."[2]

Of course, some deacons find praying the Liturgy of the Hours burdensome, at least some of the time. It can seem to be a devilish combination of complexity and monotony, as one flips back and forth seeking first the proper *Benedictus* antiphon and then the intercessions from the common of martyrs and so forth, while having to recite once again the psalms and canticle for Sunday of Week I. The psalms appointed for a particular day might seem irrelevant to my life at that moment, railing against Moab on my wedding anniversary and exulting in God's goodness on the day I receive a diagnosis of cancer. Is part of the problem that the Hours have their origin in monastic communal prayer, and deacons (as well as most priests) are non-monastics who pray the Hours alone? Is there simply a lack of fit between form and function here?

I do not think so. Once again, intelligent participation can be the key. If the deacon sees the Liturgy of the Hours as just a bunch of pious words strung together, then that toxic spiritual combination of confusion and tedium will surely result. But the church provides many resources for understanding the Hours, not least of which is the *General Instruction of the Liturgy of the Hours*, which offers not simply directions, but a whole theology of the Hours as the church's way of consecrating time to God. Let me mention just a few points that might help deacons who from time to time struggle with making the Hours a vehicle of true prayer.

First, the Hours are vocal prayer. That is, they are prayer that involves words. But because they are liturgical prayer, these words are not ones that spontaneously arise from the heart of the one praying, but are what we might call "borrowed words," words that come from without and must be interiorized. Though the church no longer requires that the words be at least whispered in order to fulfill one's obligation to recite the Hours,[3] there was a certain wisdom to this older practice since, at least in my experience, it is possible to read an entire psalm silently only to arrive at the end and discover that you have no idea what psalm it was that you just "read." Of course, pronouncing the words aloud is no guarantee that one will attend to them, but the fact of physical engagement—having the words on one's lips and tongue—can support spiritual engagement, since, as we have seen, human beings are psychosomatic unities and not simply souls inhabiting bodies. Some deacons even find it helpful to sing the Hours, or at least elements of them like the hymn and gospel canticle, during private recitation.

Further, the words of the Hours are borrowed words, but they are also alien words, not simply in the sense of being someone else's and not our own, but also in the sense of speaking of things that may seem very distant from and even repugnant to our modern sensibilities. This can be the case particularly with the psalms. Some psalms seem intent on giving us a lesson in Bronze Age history, speaking of persons long dead and kingdoms long vanished. Some express morally dubious sentiments, such as a desire to see our enemies destroyed. How can these alien words become vehicles of prayer? It was precisely in answer to such difficulties that early Christians developed what is sometimes called the "spiritual interpretation" of Scripture. This was a way of prayerfully reading the sacred text so that the things of which it spoke were seen as pointing to other realities. Thus, to borrow an example used by John Cassian (ca. 360–435), when we pray a psalm that speaks of "Jerusalem," on one level we are reading about the historical capital of the Israelite nation. But that historical reality is itself a symbol for a variety of spiritual meanings: it can symbolize the church, or our own soul, or our heavenly homeland.[4] Thus when on the Tuesday evening of the fourth week of the psalter we read in Psalm 137, "If I forget you, Jerusalem, let my right hand wither," we can pray this as not only a prayer concerned with an ancient city, but as a prayer concerning our devotion to the church, or the need to nurture our own spiritual well-being, or our desire to always remember the high destiny to which we have been called in Christ. In seeking in this way to open up the ancient words of the psalms, we are engaged in a kind of spiritual exercise by which the words of the church become our words.

The importance of the Liturgy of the Hours should also not eclipse other forms of prayer in the life of the deacon, particularly the daily Eucharist, but also devotions such as the rosary, prayerful engagement with Scripture through *lectio divina*, eucharistic adoration, and so forth. Morning and Evening Prayer can fittingly serve as the fixed poles between which these other forms of prayer are ranged.

A Liturgically Shaped Space Within

As we see already in reflecting on the Liturgy of the Hours, part of what it means to have a liturgical spirituality is to let the words and actions of the liturgy shape our interior lives. In chapter 2, speaking of the power of ritual, I noted how this power is rooted in our bodily, animal nature. It is as the union of body and soul that humans are living beings. Our bodies both give expression to the thoughts and passions of our souls and shape those thoughts and passions. Kneeling or striking one's breast can both express penitence that we already feel and help us to experience penitence that we do not yet feel. Raising our voices in song can both enable us to show the joy of the Spirit in our hearts and crack open hearts that are closed to the Spirit's joy. In other words, the liturgy is both expressive and formative; indeed, it is precisely through its expressive power that it is formative. As Louis Bouyer wrote years ago, describing the liturgical spirituality of the early church, "In the collective prayer, each took his own part and so made it his own most personal prayer; thus a prayer which was nourished by that of the whole community brought back to the prayer of the whole community the spiritual fruit which each person had derived."[5] Praying liturgically with others over the course of years, the communally expressed faith of the church works its way into our hearts and transforms them.

As Bouyer indicates, liturgy has a capacity to unite the inner and the outer, the subjective and the objective. In our culture, "spirituality" is sometimes a kind of code word for untrammeled subjectivity, as when people claim to be spiritual but not religious and mean that they believe there is something more to life than what we can see but reject any set expression of what that might be, particularly any expression rooted in a historic community or institution. There is a danger that such a spirituality detached from any tradition can become a purely individual path, locked within the self and cut off from others—perhaps, in the end, cut off even from God. But a liturgical spirituality is one that unites the inner and the outer, and can therefore save us from the awful lonely fate of being spiritual but not religious. We are not left entirely on our own to decide what the "shape" of our interior life will be, because through the liturgy over time the great tradition of the church shapes us, attunes our hearts and minds to the mind of Christ, so that our lives might become icons of his life.

How do we know that this shaping of our interior by the liturgy is happening? We might listen for resonances of the liturgy in our personal prayer lives. When calling out to God in sorrow, does our prayer echo the psalms of lament? When our hearts fill with a sense of profound gratitude, do we find the words of the *Magnificat* on our lips? When our interior life is shaped in this way, we become an echo chamber in which the psalmist's prayer and the Blessed Virgin's praise resound down through history.

We might also look for signs of an attunement of our liturgical life and our "ordinary" life. Does our liturgical celebration of baptism lead us to see each person we meet as a potential brother or sister in Christ, in whom "There is neither Jew nor Greek, there is neither slave nor free person, there is not male and female" (Gal 3:28)? Having consecrated time to God through the Liturgy of the Hours, do we treat our day as a sacred gift that God has given back to us to be used for his glory? Is the generosity of God toward us, for which we give thanks in the Eucharist and which we tangibly receive in the food and drink of Christ's Body and Blood, something that inspires us to be generous to others in return, feeding them as God has fed us? By our internalization of the divine reality that makes itself present to us in the liturgy, that same reality is borne out into the world. Bathed in the divine glory that shines upon us in the liturgy, we go in peace, glorifying the Lord by our lives.

Deacons are often asked what it is that deacons can *do*, as if their diaconal identity were simply a collection of tasks that they have been authorized to accomplish. It has become a bit of a cliché to answer that diaconal ministry is not simply a matter of *doing*, but of *being*, that it is not a job description, but an identity. Cliché or not, there is truth in this response. And in the deacon's ministry of liturgy, no less than his ministries of God's word or of charity and justice, his call is not simply to do things, and to do them well, but to be within the Body of the church in a particular sort of way. It is a call to be a person shaped by service to the liturgy, which is to be a person shaped by service to the gospel, which in turn is to be conformed to Christ through his great *leitourgia* of reconciliation.

Notes

Chapter 1

1. See P. J. Rhodes, "Who Ran Democratic Athens?," in *Polis and Politics: Studies in Ancient Greek History*, ed. Pernille Flensted-Jensen, Thomas Heine Nielsen, and Lene Rubinstein, 465–78, esp. 469–70 (Copenhagen: Museum Tusculanum Press, 2000).

2. E.g., Septuagint, Num 8:22; 16:9.

3. John N. Collins, "Theology of Ministry in the Twentieth Century: Ongoing Problems or New Orientations?," in *Diakonia Studies: Critical Issues in Ministry* (Oxford: Oxford University Press, 2014), 181.

4. *Didache* 14 (WEC 1:191). Unless otherwise noted, patristic texts are taken from Lawrence J. Johnson, *Worship in the Early Church: An Anthology of Historical Sources* (WEC), 4 vols. (Collegeville, MN: Liturgical Press, 2009), with volume and marginal paragraph number citations from that edition.

5. *Didache* 15 (WEC 1:192).

6. Ignatius of Antioch, *Letter to the Trallians* 2 (WEC 1:217).

7. Justin Martyr, *First Apology* 65; cf. 67 (WEC 1:244, 246).

8. Tertullian, *On Baptism* 17 (WEC 1:468).

9. Cyprian, *Letter* 5 (WEC 1:526).

10. Cyprian, *On the Lapsed* 25 (WEC 1:511).

11. See Paul F. Bradshaw, Maxwell E. Johnson, and L. Edward Phillips, *The Apostolic Tradition: A Commentary*, ed. Harold W. Attridge (Minneapolis: Fortress Press, 2002), 1–17.

12. *Apostolic Tradition* 8 (WEC 1:633).

13. Ibid., 4, 21 (WEC 1:622, 684).

14. Ibid., 22 (WEC 1:690).

15. Ibid., 21 (WEC 1:687).

16. Ibid., 21 (WEC 1:674, 676).

17. Ibid., 28 (WEC 1:705). On the question of who performs the actual baptism, see Bradshaw et al., *The Apostolic Tradition: A Commentary*, 125.

18. *Didascalia of the Apostles* 12 (WEC 1:768).

19. Ibid., 11 (WEC 1:767); cf. *Apostolic Constitutions* 2.54 (WEC 2:1610) and Cyril of Jerusalem, *Mystagogical Catechesis* 5.3 (WEC 2:2146).

20. *The Canons of Father Athanasius*, canon 57 (WEC 2:2447).

21. Ibid., canon 27 (WEC 2:2434).

22. *Apostolic Constitutions* 2.57 (WEC 2:1612).

23. Ibid., 2.57 (WEC 2:1615); cf. 8.10 (WEC 2:1713–33). The role of the deacon in leading the various litanies and other forms of the intercessions in the Eucharist and other liturgies is well attested; see John Chrysostom, *Homily 2 on the Obscurity of Prophecies* 5 (WEC 2:1540); Egeria, *Pilgrimage to the Holy Places* 24:5-6 (WEC 2:2166); Augustine, Letter 55 (WEC 3:2626).

24. *Apostolic Constitutions* 2.57 (WEC 2:1614); 8.12 (WEC 2:1743).

25. Ibid., 8.13 (WEC 2:1787).

26. Ibid., 8.15 (WEC 2:1793).

27. Ibid., 8.9 (WEC 2:1711).

28. Ibid., 8.12 (WEC 2:1743).

29. Ibid., 8.46 (WEC 2:1854).

30. Council of Nicaea, canon 18 (WEC 2:1455).

31. *Canons of Hippolytus*, canon 31 (WEC 2:2322).

32. Ibid., canon 30 (WEC 2:2321).

33. Second Synod of Arles, canon 15 (WEC 3:3144).

34. Pope Gelasius, Letter 14 (WEC 3:2927).

35. *De Septem Ordinibus Ecclesiae* 5 (WEC 3:3042).

36. *Testamentum Domini* 2.10 (WEC 3:3828).

37. Synod of Dvin, canon 18 (WEC 4:4845).

38. Pope Gelasius, Letter 14 (WEC 3:2927).

39. Jerome, *Dialogue Between a Luciferian and an Orthodox Christian* 9 (WEC 3:3930).

40. Canon 16 (WEC 4:4599).

41. *De Septem Ordinibus Ecclesiae* 6 (WEC 3:3043).

42. For a discussion of deacons as ministers of Communion in the early church, with an eye toward reforming current Orthodox practice, see Paul L. Gavrilyuk, "The Role of Deacons in the Distribution of Communion in the Early Church," *St. Vladimir's Theological Quarterly* 51/2–3 (2007): 255–75.

43. Synod of Rome of 595, canon 1 (WEC 4:4226). On deacons as singers, see Christopher Page, *The Christian West and Its Singers: The First Thousand Years* (New Haven, CT: Yale University Press, 2010), 155–71.

44. See *Canons of Hippolytus*, canon 37, which mentions special white vestments worn by the deacons, presbyters, and bishop (WEC 2:2336).

45. Theodore of Mopsuestia, Homily 15 (WEC 3:3438).

46. Theodor Klauser comments at the end of a description of an eighth-century papal Mass, "we can scarcely recognize this overburdened liturgy for

what it was supposed to be—an imitation and recalling of that simple memorial meal instituted by Our Lord" (*A Short History of the Western Liturgy: An Account and Some Reflections*, trans. John Halliburton [Oxford: Oxford University Press, 1969], 69).

47. See the discussion in Page, *The Christian West and Its Singers*, 206–7.

48. See Augustine Thompson, *Cities of God: The Religion of the Italian Communes, 1125–1325* (University Park, PA: Pennsylvania State University Press, 2005), 240.

49. John Bossy, *Christianity in the West: 1400–1700* (Oxford: Oxford University Press, 1985), 66.

50. Augustine Thompson, OP, personal correspondence with the author, July 22, 2015.

51. With slight variations, the pseudo-Isidorian account is found in Hugh of St. Victor (1096–1141), *De Sacramentis* 2.3.10; Peter Lombard (1100–1160), *Sententiae* bk. 4, distinction 24, ch. 10, n. 2; and William Durand (1230–96), *Rationale divinorum officiorum* 2.9.10.

52. *Epistola Beati Isidori Ivnioris ad Leudefredum* in *Conciliorvm Omnivm Generalivm Et Provincialivm Collectio Regia*, vol. 15 (Paris: Typographia Regia, 1644), 338.

53. See, e.g., Thomas Aquinas (1225–74), *Summa Contra Gentiles* 4.75.3.

54. See Thompson, *Cities of God*, 27. Some in the West, however, still maintained that deacons, like laypersons, should only perform emergency baptisms.

55. Gratian, *Decretum*, Book IV, title 1, case 9 (Friedberg ed.).

56. An exception would be the Church of England, which retained the threefold ministry of deacon, bishop, and priest.

57. Council of Trent, Session 23, Decree on the Sacrament of Orders: Decree on Reform, canon 17.

58. Ibid., Decree on the Sacrament of Orders, chap. 2.

59. Ibid., Decree on the Sacrament of Orders: Decree on Reform, canon 18.

60. One elderly priest, ordained before the Second Vatican Council, recounted to me how he had been ordained a subdeacon on one day, a deacon on the next, and a priest on the third.

61. See Josef A. Jungmann, SJ, *The Mass of the Roman Rite: Its Origins and Development (Missarum Sollemnia)*, 2 vols., trans. F. Brunner (Notre Dame, IN: Christian Classics, 1951), vol. 1, 206–7.

62. See, e.g., Karl Rahner, "The Theology of the Restoration of the Diaconate," in *Theological Investigations V: Later Writings*, trans. Karl-H. Kruger (New York: Crossroad, 1966), 268–314, esp. 282–83.

63. Jungmann, *The Mass of the Roman Rite*, vol. 1, 165.

64. Quotations from the Second Vatican Council are taken from Austin Flannery, ed., *Vatican Council II: Constitutions, Decrees, Declarations; The Basic Sixteen Documents* (Collegeville, MN: Liturgical Press, 2014).

Chapter 2

1. Thomas Aquinas, *Summa Theologiae* III, q. 61, a. 1.

2. Aidan Kavanagh, *Elements of Rite: A Handbook of Liturgical Style* (Collegeville, MN: Liturgical Press, 1990), 76; cf. GIRM 94.

3. While the master of ceremonies at an episcopal liturgy is often a priest, it is arguably more fitting that a deacon fulfill that function, given his role in the liturgy generally. The *Ceremonial of Bishops* perhaps reflects the deacon's normative role as master of ceremonies in specifying that, while a priest serving in that role wears a cassock and surplice (thus masking his priestly identity), the deacon may wear the dalmatic, the distinctive vestment of his order (36).

4. For a particularly sharp rebuke of this practice, see *Redemptionis Sacramentum* 59.

5. See *Ceremonial of Bishops* 107.

6. Augustine, *The City of God* 19.17.

7. Christopher Page, *The Christian West and Its Singers: The First Thousand Years* (New Haven, CT: Yale University Press, 2010), 155–56.

8 *Summa Theologiae* II-II, q. 91, a. 1.

9. Exceptions would be "devotional" prayers prescribed by the liturgy that are intended to be said inaudibly, such as the words as the deacon kisses the Book of the Gospels at the end of the reading or at the mixing of water into the chalice.

10. "In texts that are to be pronounced in a loud and clear voice . . . the voice should correspond to the genre of the text itself, that is, depending upon whether it is a reading, a prayer, an explanatory comment, an acclamation, or a sung text; it should also be suited to the form of celebration and to the solemnity of the gathering" (GIRM 38).

11. Kavanagh, *Elements of Rite*, 32.

12. See *Musicam Sacram* 7; GIRM 40.

13. *De Ecclesiasticis Officiis* 1.5, quoted in Page, *The Christian West and Its Singers*, 40.

14. For more extensive advice on singing the ministerial chants, see International Commission on English in the Liturgy, *Chants of the Roman Missal: Study Edition* (Collegeville, MN: Liturgical Press, 2012), 9–16.

15. See GIRM 335; cf. Robert Hovda, "The Vesting of Liturgical Ministers," *Worship* 54 (1980): 98–117.

16. Some deacons also wear an amice (a cloth that goes around the neck when using an alb that does not fit closely at the top) and a cincture (the rope that goes around the waist on top of the alb, often unflattering on middle-aged men).

17. "It is praiseworthy to refrain from exercising the option of omitting the dalmatic" (*Redemptionis Sacramentum* 125).

18. The last instance is specified in the 1990 *editio typica altera* n. 80.

19. Or cassock and surplice, though in my experience these are rarely worn by deacons.

20. *Canons of Father Athanasius*, canon 106 (WEC 2:2461).

21. *Ceremonial of Bishops* 91–93.

Chapter 3

1. Though they can tend to creep into the liturgy. The old "Prayers at the Foot of the Altar" of the preconciliar Mass originated as the private preparation of the ministers.

2. GIRM 120, 172. Note that the Lectionary is not to be carried in procession.

3. See GIRM 173, 274. If the tabernacle is in the sanctuary but not situated directly behind the altar, the minsters might first bow to the altar and then genuflect to the Sacrament. The deacon should probably simply follow local custom.

4. GIRM 174. Despite the rubrics, some celebrants lead the Introductory Rites from the altar. In those cases, the deacon should stand with the celebrant, on his right, and perhaps look for some future occasion to chat with the priest about rubrics and why they matter.

5. Michael Kwatera, *The Liturgical Ministry of Deacons* (Collegeville, MN: Liturgical Press, 2005), 32; Paul Turner, *Let Us Pray: A Guide to the Rubrics of Sunday Mass* (Collegeville, MN: Liturgical Press, 2012), 52.

6. Introduction to the Lectionary 42.

7. GIRM 176; see the principles articulated in GIRM 91.

8. Turner, *Let Us Pray*, 73.

9. *Ceremonial of Bishops* 141.

10. GIRM 136. Paul Turner notes that though the celebrant has the option of preaching from his chair, the deacon should probably not do so, since the deacon's chair "does not hold the same liturgical weight as the presider's" (*Let Us Pray*, 77).

11. GIRM 177. Though other places for offering the intentions are given for other ministers, only the ambo is mentioned for the deacon.

12. GIRM 177. For the nomenclature, see the Roman Missal, Order of Mass 20.

13. Mass for the 30th Sunday of the Year, October 28, 2012, http://www.vatican.va/news_services/liturgy/libretti/2012/20121028.pdf.

14. GIRM 139. If Communion is to be given under both species, there may be multiple chalices and purificators, and if there is not sufficient room for the chalices on the corporal, there may be additional corporals. On the optional use of the pall, see n. 118c.

15. GIRM 178. A server can also cense the celebrant(s) and assembly.

16. *Ceremonial of Bishops* 153.

17. Ibid., 155.

18. See Aidan Kavanagh, *Elements of Rite: A Handbook of Liturgical Style* (Collegeville, MN: Liturgical Press, 1990), 76.

19. Note, however, that the *Directory for Masses with Children* does allow, and even encourage, free adaptation of this invitation (23).

20. GIRM 83; *Redemptionis Sacramentum* 73.

21. *Norms for the Distribution and Reception of Holy Communion under Both Kinds in the Dioceses of the United States of America* 37.

22. *Sacrosanctum Concilium* 55; *Redemptionis Sacramentum* 89; GIRM 85; *Norms for the Distribution and Reception of Holy Communion* 30.

23. GIRM 242; *Redemptionis Sacramentum* 98.

24. GIRM 182. The *Ceremonial of Bishops*, after describing the Communion of the deacons, states that concelebrants "go up to the altar and receive the blood of the Lord from a deacon" (164), implying that concelebrants receive the cup after the deacon.

25. *Norms for the Distribution and Reception of Holy Communion* 45.

26. *Norms for the Distribution and Reception of Holy Communion* 50; *Redemptionis Sacramentum* 104.

27. The statement is in a 2014 addendum to his 1972 article, "Zur Frage nach der Unauflöslichkeit der Ehe. Bemerkungen zum dogmengeschichtlichen Befund und zu seiner gegenwärtigen Bedeutung," prepared for republication in his *opera omnia*. The text of the addendum can be found in Sandro Magister, "In the Synod on the Family Even the Pope Emeritus Is Speaking Out," http://chiesa.espresso.repubblica.it/articolo/1350933?eng=y, retrieved July 28, 2015.

28. *Norms for the Distribution and Reception of Holy Communion* 52.

29. Instituted acolytes, however, are permitted to purify the vessels. See GIRM 279.

30. GIRM 163. Even for priests, purifying the vessels at the credence table is preferred. See GIRM 279.

31. GIRM 185. The *Ceremonial of Bishops* says that he may "use similar words" (169).

Chapter 4

1. Code of Canon Law, c. 866.

2. RCIA 372; for the rite, see 340–69.

3. RCIA 375–86, 393–99.

4. RCIA 226. By "a great number" the rite presumably means scores of people, not nine or ten.

5. In proposing this way of looking at the RCIA, I am giving priority to the second way of conceiving it found in the introduction to the rite (7) rather than the first (6); were I discussing the RCIA from the perspective of the deacon's ministry of the Word, I might well reverse that order of priority.

6. National Statutes for the Catechumenate 10.

7. Code of Canon Law, c. 206, c. 1183 §1; National Statutes for the Catechumenate 9.

8. Option A in RCIA 102 seems the most suitable, but particularly if the anointing is repeated numerous times, the presider may wish to use one of the prayers in RCIA 94.

9. RCIA 117. Note that if both the prayer of the faithful and the profession of faith are used, the profession follows the intercessions, rather than preceding them as it normally does.

10. Roman Missal, Easter Vigil 39. While it might seem appropriate for the deacon to carry the paschal candle in this procession, since he is the one who has carried it into the church at the beginning of the Vigil, the *Ceremonial of Bishops* (358) specifies that "an acolyte" carry the candle.

11. The National Statutes for the Catechumenate (16) and the current edition of the Roman Missal (Easter Vigil 48) are in conflict over whether there can be an anointing with the oil of catechumens between the renunciation of sin and the profession of faith. Presumably this discrepancy will be clarified at some point. If an anointing takes place, it would be appropriate for the deacon to hold the vessel of oil while the celebrant performs the anointing.

12. *Ceremonial of Bishops* 365. Paul Turner speculates that the point is to visually distinguish the anointing of the infants from the confirmation of the adults, which would follow shortly. See *Glory in the Cross: Holy Week in the Third Edition of the Roman Missal* (Collegeville, MN: Liturgical Press, 2011), 153–54. If this is the case, then it might be appropriate at a Vigil where the priest presider will confirm the newly baptized adults for the deacon to anoint the infants while the priest speaks the formula for anointing.

13. The RCIA (231) says that confirmation may be administered either at the font or in the sanctuary; the Roman Missal (Easter Vigil 53) specifies that it should be done in the sanctuary.

14. The Roman Missal (Easter Vigil 49, 55) mentions the possibility of the assembly renewing its promises immediately after the elect have professed their faith, prior to their baptism. If this option is used, it is not clear when, or if, the assembly would be sprinkled with the baptismal water.

15. Roman Missal, Easter Vigil 57.

16. National Statutes for the Catechumenate 26, 33.

17. See Everett Ferguson, *Baptism in the Early Church: History, Theology, and Liturgy in the First Five Centuries* (Grand Rapids, MI: Eerdmans, 2009), 362–79, 629.

18. *Book of Blessings*, General Introduction 18. For this reference and its application I am indebted to Paul Turner, "Deacons and Baptism," http://paulturner.org/deacons-and-baptism/, retrieved July 28, 2015.

19. See *Christian Initiation*, General Introduction 33.

20. Of course, much will depend on the specific layout of the particular building, as well as the size and composition of the assembly.

21. Feast of the Baptism of the Lord, Mass and Administration of the Sacrament of Baptism: Homily of Pope Francis, Sistine Chapel, 12 January 2014, http://w2.vatican.va/content/francesco/en/homilies/2014/documents/papa-francesco_20140112_omelia-battesimo.html.

22. Somewhat oddly, the first two forms of blessing direct the celebrant to touch the water while the third indicates that he is to make the sign of the cross. This is perhaps because only the third form actually uses the term "bless."

23. Roman Missal, Easter Vigil 44. The *Rite of Baptism for Children* has not been recently retranslated, so the wording of this prayer differs between it and the Missal. Presumably either form may be used.

24. RBC 57–58. Again, a different translation is found in the Roman Missal (Easter Vigil 55).

25. *Christian Initiation*, General Introduction 22.

26. Simply dipping the child's bottom in the water is both insufficient as a sign and of dubious validity.

27. The rite prefers the parents hold the child, but acknowledges that in some cultures this role might be taken by the godparents (RBC 60).

28. For how baptism is integrated into the Sunday Eucharist, see RBC 29.

29. Note that this differs from baptism celebrated outside of Mass, where only the parents and godparents respond to the questions.

Chapter 5

1. Though see GILH 258 on how the celebration differs when a layperson presides.

2. See *Ceremonial of Bishops* 196.

3. One resource including everything needed for chanting Morning and Evening Prayer to simple tones is *The Mundelein Psalter* (Chicago: Liturgy Training Publications, 2007).

4. See the United States complementary norm to canon 766: http://www.usccb.org/beliefs-and-teachings/what-we-believe/canon-law/complementary-norms/canon-766-lay-preaching.cfm.

5. GILH 261; *Ceremonial of Bishops* 203–4.

6. For details, see GILH 93–99.

7. *Ceremonial of Bishops* 205, 207.

8. Different dioceses have different policies regarding when such celebrations can take place; deacons should, of course, follow their diocesan policy.

9. USCCB, *Gathered in Steadfast Faith* 62, in *Sunday Celebrations in the Absence of a Priest* (Washington, DC: USCCB, 2007).

10. See http://www.usccb.org/prayer-and-worship/the-mass/frequently-asked-questions/weekday-celebrations-in-the-absence-of-a-priest.cfm, retrieved July 28, 2015. Presumably this would include the special opening prayer, the thanksgiving after Communion, and the various references to the priest's absence.

11. The translation of the rite dates from 1974; presumably the English translations currently used at Mass should be substituted for those found in the ritual book.

12. *Holy Communion and Worship of the Eucharist Outside Mass* 29.

13. Ibid., 80.

14. The Eucharist can also be exposed in a ciborium, though in my experience this is rarely done.

15. *Holy Communion and Worship of the Eucharist Outside Mass* 93.

16. Ibid., 97.

17. *Ceremonial of Bishops* 1108–9, 1113–14.

Chapter 6

1. See Corinna Laughlin, "Introduction," in *Proclamations for Christmas, Epiphany, and Easter* (Chicago: Liturgy Training Publications, 2011), vii.

2. For example, http://www.catholicculture.org/culture/liturgicalyear/prayers/view.cfm?id=48. Taken from Philip T. Weller, *Roman Ritual: Volume III, The Blessings* (Bruce Publishing, 1952).

3. After Vatican II the crowd's part was often given to the assembly; some people feel that calling out "crucify him" is one of the most meaningful parts of Holy Week, and others question the appropriateness of such "audience participation."

4. See Paul Turner, *Glory in the Cross: Holy Week in the Third Edition of the Roman Missal* (Collegeville, MN: Liturgical Press, 2011), 17.

5. *Blessing of Oils and Consecration of the Chrism* 16–18; the role of the deacons is stated somewhat more clearly in the *Ceremonial of Bishops* 282, 284.

6. *Blessing of Oils and Consecration of the Chrism* 20, 27.

7. *Universal Norms on the Liturgical Year and the General Roman Calendar* 18.

8. Congregation for Divine Worship, *Paschalis Sollemnitatis* 45.

9. Roman Missal, Thursday of the Lord's Supper 10.

10. *Ceremonial of Bishops* 307; Roman Missal, Thursday of the Lord's Supper 38.

11. Roman Missal, Thursday of the Lord's Supper 39.

12. See Congregation for Divine Worship, *Paschalis Sollemnitatis* 40. Since the evening Mass of the Lord's Supper is the only Mass in parishes on Holy Thursday, it might be good to celebrate the morning Office on that day as well.

13. Ibid., 72.

14. Roman Missal, Friday of the Passion of the Lord 4.

15. Ibid., 10. The rubric states that the priest gives a homily. It is not clear whether this is meant to exclude the deacon preaching on Good Friday. It is possible that the intention was to make clear that even though this is not a Mass, it is not an occasion on which a layperson should be invited to give a reflection.

16. See the *Ceremonial of Bishops* 319.

17. Roman Missal, Friday of the Passion of the Lord 15.

18. The rubrics say that the priest might also do this, but this would presumably refer to occasions when no deacon is present. See ibid., 16.

19. See the direction in the *Ceremonial of Bishops* 343.

20. Though the text is presented both with and without music, it is difficult to imagine the *Exsultet* being read instead of sung.

21. For a discussion, see Laughlin, "Introduction," in *Proclamations for Christmas, Epiphany, and Easter*, vii–viii.

22. Texts for home blessing during Easter season are provided in the *Book of Blessings*.

Chapter 7

1. The rite for two baptized people allows for Communion to be given from the reserved sacrament (OCM 108–115), but most dioceses forbid this practice.

2. *Ceremonial of Bishops* 500, 524.

3. Ibid., 507, 529; likewise at the ordination of a bishop (580).

4. See, most recently, the 2005 Note on the Minister of the Sacrament of the Anointing of the Sick, by the Congregation for the Doctrine of the Faith, http://www.vatican.va/roman_curia/congregations/cfaith/documents/rc_con_cfaith_doc_20050211_unzione-infermi_en.html.

5. See also Genevieve Glen, OSB, "Going Forth in the Spirit, the Road Before Us," in *Recovering the Riches of Anointing: A Study of the Sacrament of the Sick*, ed. Genevieve Glen, 113–30, esp. 120–21 (Collegeville, MN: Liturgical Press, 2002).

6. USCCB Committee on Divine Worship, *Newsletter*, January 2012.

Chapter 8

1. One wonders how many deacons when out of town on a Sunday use this directive to inflict themselves on an unsuspecting celebrant.

2. *General Instruction of the Liturgy of the Hours* 28.

3. *Notitiae* 9 (1973): 150.

4. John Cassian, *Conferences*, conf. 14, chap. 8.

5. Louis Bouyer, *Liturgical Piety* (Notre Dame, IN: University of Notre Dame Press, 1955), 243.